Children playing football in the playground, as documented for the 'Fazimentos' publications produced by the Fundação Darcy Ribeiro

Wherever You Find People

The Radical Schools of Oscar Niemeyer, Darcy Ribeiro and Leonel Brizola

 PARK BOOKS

Aberrant Architecture

Chapter 1
In The Rear-View Mirror

9	Foreword, Vicky Richardson
13	Animating Education, Aberrant Architecture
19	Schools That Are (like) Wings, Ligia Nobre
22	Learning By Numbers: Map of CIEPs
25	Why Build Public Schools? Shumi Bose
29	Inventing Other Stories: A Conversation with Aberrant Architecture

Chapter 2
Fazimentos: Those Who Did

41	Leonel Brizola, The State Governor
43	Carmen Rangel & Laurinda Barbosa, The Coordinators

Chapter 3
A Fabric Of Schools

63	Oscar Niemeyer, The Architect
65	Washington Fajardo, The Urban Planner
77	Ricardo Henriques, The Economist
81	Carlos Niemeyer, The Archivist
87	Lauro Cavalcanti, The Curator

Chapter 4
The Equation To Be Solved

95	José Carlos Süssekind, The Engineer
99	Jair Valera, The Architect

Chapter 5

The Pedagogical Adventure

| 109 | Darcy Ribeiro, The Anthropologist |

Chapter 6

The School Is Yours

127	Carmen Barretto, The Teacher
137	Renata Carneiro, The Director
143	Leonardo Peixoto & Silvestre, The Teacher & The Social Parent

Chapter 7

The CIEP Is The Channel

| 159 | Lenita Vilela, The Director |
| 171 | Carlos Eduardo, The Policeman |

Chapter 8

This Idea, It's Magic.

179	Claudia Costin & Rafael Parente, The Politicians
185	Can Good Architecture Be One-Size-Fits-All?
	Alastair Donald, Aberrant Architecture
189	Always More To Learn, Aberrant Architecture
193	Postscript, Beatrice Galilee

| 195 | Acknowledgements |

Chapter 1
In the Rear-View Mirror

The swimming pool at the CIEP Ayrton Senna Da Silva in the São Conrado neighbourhood, named for Brazil's legendary Formula One driver

Aberrant Architecture presented their research on the CIEPs at the 2012 Venice Architecture Biennale in a display entitled Animating Education

Foreword
> Vicky Richardson

Like Aberrant, the first time I saw a CIEP *(Centros Integrados de Educação Pública)* was from a speeding car. On a visit to Rio in 2011, I drove past a painted blue one and my *British Council* colleague, Cristina Bokel Becker, mentioned that the distinctive building was a type of school that offered round-the-clock childcare. I was deeply impressed with this fact, having three small children at the time, though I was unaware that these schools had a particular architectural philosophy and were designed by Oscar Niemeyer.

The significance of the CIEPs programme only really hit home in 2012 when *Aberrant Architecture* submitted an entry to our competition for the British Pavilion at the *Venice Architecture Biennale*. Curator Vanessa Norwood and I issued an open call for examples of architectural innovation from overseas that the UK could learn from. We selected 10 teams and gave them each a travel grant to 'bring back ideas to change British architecture'. *Venice Takeaway* overturned the tradition of a national pavilion by showing ideas from the rest of the world and emphasising universal values.

In 2012, with the London Olympic Games approaching, all eyes seemed to be on the UK and so we thought it was a good time to look further afield. The subject of school design was particularly urgent: the British government had cancelled a programme called 'Building Schools for the Future' and there seemed to be a dearth of big thinking on the subject.

The CIEP programme itself was the victim of political change, having been cancelled in 1994 after a ten year spurt of activity. Its rapidity, design and construction methods were in part derived from the need to make an impact within a term of political office (in fact the CIEPs programme managed to endure two terms). But this observation of its pragmatism is not intended to diminish its achievement, and in the UK we still have so much to learn from this brave, humanist idea.

In 1984 the CIEPs were a new building type, driven by the ambition to bring the best quality design to the largest number; and to create civic buildings that would inspire people in self-built communities with the potential of having more and better. To say that the hundreds of CIEPs were churned out over a few short years is not a criticism. Their pre-fabricated concrete construction was designed to ensure quality and cost efficiencies at large volume. Oscar Niemeyer—working with a visionary client-partnership in the shape of Darcy Ribeiro, a noted sociologist, and Leonel Brizola who was then Governor of the State of Rio—conceived a brilliant set of modular elements so that the CIEPs could be customised for each locality. The range of facilities they offered made them a beacon of hope.

Aberrant brought all this to our attention in 2012 within the British Pavilion, where they created a stunning installation representing all 508 CIEPs as 1:500 cast models, each with a label describing its location. The following year, the exhibition moved to the *RIBA Gallery* in central London, and in 2013 the installation travelled to Brazil to be shown at the *X São Paulo Architecture Biennial*. All the while, Aberrant has continued to explore the ideas of the CIEPs in its own work—for example at the Rosemary Works Primary School in De Beauvoir Town—and to deepen their research in looking at the design of CIEP furniture and community engagement. In 2014 the *Museu de Arte do Rio* (MAR) acquired the installation as part of its permanent collection. In the same year, another travel grant allowed Aberrant to return to Rio, investigating the convivial spaces of a traditional Afro-Brazilian 'jongo' music school in the Morro da Serrinha favela in Madureira; most recently in 2016, a further workshop developed furniture for the *Escolinha Tia Percilia*, an independent school in Babilônia.

Despite the current political and economic crisis in Brazil, there are positive moves to rediscover CIEPs, and to embrace their transformative ideals. Here in the UK, it may take us a little longer. Four years that have passed since *Aberrant* began their research on CIEPs; this has also been a symbolically important period in which the Olympic torch has been handed from London to Rio. In September 2012, the British Council opened *Transform,* a four-year cultural season, with an exhibition about the great Brazilian architect Lina Bo Bardi. *Transform* aimed to highlight the potential of art to change lives, and at the same time to draw British artists and architects into a closer relationship with Brazil. Aberrant's work on the CIEPs is a wonderful example of these aspirations and a reminder of the transformative potential of architecture.

Vicky Richardson
Commissioner of the British Pavilion, Venice Architecture Biennale 2010–2016

Vicky Richardson was Director of Architecture, Design & Fashion at the British Council (2010–2015), the UK's leading international institution for educational opportunities and cultural relations. During this time she was instrumental in hosting many international cultural initiatives and events, among them the exhibition Lina Bo Bardi: Together in 2012. In the same year, she co-curated Venice Takeaway, for the British Pavilion at the 13th Venice Biennale of Architecture, commissioning Aberrant Architecture as one of twelve practices to research innovative architectural ideas from around the globe.

Aberrant Architecture's Animating Education installation included a scale model of every CIEP, individually labelled with its name and location

CIEPs are often located on difficult sites, for example along the Linha Vermelha expressway, connecting São João de Meriti and Rio de Janeiro

Animating Education: Learning From Rio De Janeiro
Aberrant Architecture

Prologue: Pre-School

On the long flight from London to Rio de Janeiro, we dipped into a copy of *Curves of Time*, the memoirs of Oscar Niemeyer—Brazil's most famous, cherished and revered architect. We were flying to Rio to see what lessons we could bring back to the UK from the Niemeyer-designed *Integrated Centres of Public Education* (CIEPs), an experimental educational project conceived in 1982 by the governor of the state of Rio de Janeiro, Leonel Brizola, and his vice-governor, the Brazilian anthropologist and intellectual Darcy Ribeiro. The pair facilitated a network of 508 CIEPs schools, which now cover the entire state, giving children from under-privileged backgrounds 'the hope of some day having access to what only the rich enjoy today', as Niemeyer writes near the end of his memoir. The late architect is often admired for his highly inventive organic forms that reinterpret the austerity of European modernism, but this subtle statement points towards the agenda behind one of the lesser-known projects in his extensive body of work. Niemeyer was talking about the CIEPs. For us, this remark revealed much about the man and the significance of our research.

Lesson One: History

A taxi-ride through the winding narrow streets of Santa Teresa brought us to the calm surroundings of the *Fundação Darcy Ribeiro* (Darcy Ribeiro Foundation), high up in the hills above the late summer haze that typically settles over downtown Rio de Janeiro.

Inside, Laurinda Barbosa and Carmen Rangel, representatives from the Foundation and former teachers who worked with Ribeiro from the beginning of the CIEPs project, explained that in the early 1980s, 'there was a crisis with public education, especially in urban centres'. In Rio state, mass migration from the countryside to the cities swelled the urban population. Yet public schools at the time were unequipped to educate a rural population that did not share the same aptitudes, points of view or cultural background as the established metropolitan residents.

Brazil itself was also at a crossroads. The end of military dictatorship and the eager transition to democracy prompted an amnesty that allowed politicians and intellectuals to return from abroad. In Rio, free elections were held for governors. Responding to the education crisis, the new state governor implemented the construction of 508 CIEPs, which were built in towns, cities, favelas and beach resorts across Rio.

These schools were designed as 'custom-made infrastructure to support a radical, full-time education programme', according to Washington Fajardo, the Rio City Secretary of Heritage, Architecture and Design at the Secretariat for Culture. Nearly three decades later, the CIEPs project—or at least its distinctive architectural legacy—is well known to Cariocas (Rio inhabitants) and Brazilians in general. According to Fajardo, 'Wherever you find people, you'll find a CIEP.'

Lesson Two: Philosophy

The facets of the 1980s crisis of Rio's state-funded primary education were numerous: too few schools, overcrowded classrooms, high student-to-teacher ratios, scarcity of funds, lack of support, not to mention a growing gulf between private and public schools. At the Darcy Ribeiro Foundation, Barbosa and Rangel explained that the objective of the project 'was to get the new migrant population to integrate and prepare this new wave of youngsters from the countryside to ascend into urban society.'

Rio's existing public schools did not run a full-time schedule, and classes mostly addressed traditional skills like literacy and numeracy. This suited the 20% of children from the existing urban middle class, whose parents could also afford to send them to the cinema, theatre, museums, provide access to doctors, dentists and take their families on foreign holidays. However, the structure failed the 80% of rural interlopers, typically from impoverished backgrounds, who had limited access to culture and leisure facilities. In their home environments, the children of rural migrants did not receive the same level of cultural stimulus as their middle-class peers. According to Barbosa and Rangel, 'these new students needed different types of incentives.'

Thus the radical proposal at the heart of the CIEPs project envisioned schools on a grand scale, considering a multitude of aspects within the remit of 'education'—from the infrastructural scale of ambition, to the length of the academic day and how local culture could aid academic learning. Under the CIEPs programme, school would become full-time and more expansive in its provision. Children would be encouraged to learn practical skills whilst pursuing traditional academic studies. They would have access to new cultural facilities, balanced meals and recreation. Morning sessions would begin at seven in the morning and end at five in the afternoon, with evening sessions running from six to ten in the late evening. Approximately 600 students would attend morning classes, and 400 children would be enrolled for the evening.

Once the proposal was established, Ribeiro needed Rio's teaching faculty to support the programme. To this end, he put together a team to write 12 theses that set out the case for the CIEPs. This collective academic treatise drew from influences that Ribeiro had been exposed to over the years—from French education specialists, to North American concepts on pragmatic education and hands-on learning.

The theses were distributed across the state to approximately 2,500 schools, where the proposed ideas were considered by teachers and school boards. Each school subsequently sent a delegate to attend a meeting in Mendes, a town about 90km from Rio de Janeiro. Here, Ribeiro's proposal was discussed and debated until a consensus was reached on how to move forward. 'The importance of Mendes is that it was the culmination of a process of approval from the education community in relation to the project', observed Barbosa and Rangel. At the time, the Mendes meeting was described as 'a revolution in Brazilian education'.

Lesson Three: Art And Design

We met Washington Fajardo, Rio City Secretary of Heritage, Architecture and Design, in his offices in the Laranjeiras neighbourhood of Rio de Janeiro. There, he busily sketched out the architecture of a typical CIEP. 'It's a concentration of a city', he explained. 'You have the basic building, and then you have a series of associated buildings: an outdoor covered sports hall, an octagon-shaped library and a house on the roof for live-in pupils.' Some CIEPS even have outdoor swimming pools.

Our first visit to one of these 'concentrated cities' was the *CIEP Presidente Tancredo Neves* in Catete—which happens to be the first CIEP ever constructed, in 1985. The main block contains 18 classrooms of various sizes. Each classroom is marked by bright yellow furniture, specially designed for the CIEPs. Interestingly, every classroom was originally designed to support a wall mounted television for teachers and students, to learn the then-relatively new visual language of mass-media communication.

At the CIEP Tancredo Neves, an expansive covered arcade takes up the ground floor of the main block. The space is used for exhibitions, events, and also acts as a sheltered playground during Rio's seasonal bouts of intense tropical rain.

To the right of the arcade are the canteen and kitchen, where children eat three meals a day—carefully prepared by a nutritionist to ensure a healthy, balanced diet—a particularly philanthropic idea in the 1980s. On the left is the medical office. Originally, each CIEP also featured a dental facility that was staffed twice a week by a qualified dentist. Students were even allocated time for regular showers.

On the playground, we walked past the outdoor sports hall, covered by a canopy and flanked by bleacher-style seating. Nearby is the octagon-shaped library building and a beautifully shaped water tower, which ensures a constant supply to the school.

The most surprising feature of the CIEP Tancredo Neves is its student housing. Small residential blocks—one for girls and one for boys—are located on the roof of the CIEP. Some students live there during the school week, returning to their family homes on weekends. Although our visit coincided with an Easter party, some very excited children were only too happy to show us around their home. The boys' house features a living room, kitchen, bathroom, utility room and private roof terrace. The bedroom contained bright yellow bunk beds from the same furniture family as the desks and chairs found in the classrooms. Plenty of soft furnishings and other personalised fixtures contrast well with Niemeyer's modernist architecture.

Lesson Four: Resistant Materials

Oscar Niemeyer's office is located in downtown Rio and looks out past Guanabara Bay, towards Sugarloaf Mountain. Over the past three decades the designs for a majority of Niemeyer's buildings have been realised in this space. The office of the 105-year-old Niemeyer is run by his right-hand man—the architect Jair Valera—and Niemeyer's granddaughter, Ana Elisa. Standing in his office, Valera recounted that throughout the process of designing the CIEPs, 'Oscar Niemeyer and Darcy Ribeiro influenced one another. The architecture and the curriculum went very much hand-in-hand.' Ribeiro believed that everything started with education and 'that this educational system would be the salvation of the country,' and was insistent on the need for an integral full-time educational programme. Meanwhile, Niemeyer influenced Ribeiro, showing how the architecture could support and adapt to academic goals.

Valera recalled that replication was the most important aspect of the CIEPs. They had to be, 'easy to build and easy to multiply in the smallest amount of time.' Brizola and Ribeiro wanted to make ambitious structural changes, but the pair only had a four-year term in which to realise their vision. They were determined that electoral turnover would not be a barrier to the project's realisation. As a result, Niemeyer collaborated with engineer José Carlos Süssekind to design an entire, prefabricated school system. With the backing of Brizola and Ribeiro, the architect and engineer won the support of Rio's big contractors. Subsequently, the state was carved up into lots, and each contractor was allocated a certain number of schools to build.

A central factory called the *Fábrica de Escolas* was opened in the centre of Rio to manufacture the CIEP components. Each factory-made component was then taken to the sites where they were fitted together. The construction process was very quick: an entire CIEP could be built to be up and running, serving up to a thousand students each day, in just six months. In the first four years, approximately 250 schools were built, and about 250 more were constructed during Brizola's second term in office. 'Very few parts were required and the quantity of parts was small in relation to the number of schools built,' said Valera. 'More than a hundred people were employed to check the works to ensure the same quality level across all the sites and to ensure as much standardisation as possible.'

Like most new buildings in Brazil at the time, the CIEPs were primarily built using concrete. This enabled towns to contract local construction companies with the relevant skills and experience. Valera adds that concrete was also used because of its durability and flexibility in application. When considering materials, concrete was 'stronger, more solid and more resistant. The design could fit in all types of terrain.'

CIEPs are regularly found in a variety of strategic and visible locations—along freeways, in the middle of city squares, or in elevated positions such as mountainsides. These diverse locations meant that flexibility was an important building factor, with the standardised elements configured in different ways to create site-specific solutions. Three main variations were created: smaller sites consisted of a main building with a sports hall on the roof; on medium-sized sites, a library supplemented the main building and rooftop hall, while large sites incorporated an additional full-size, stand-alone hall.

Today, more than three decades after the first CIEPs were built, they remain in reasonable shape. As Ricardo Henrique—president of the urban advisory *Instituto Pereira Passos*—notes, 'they have been completely incorporated into the urban space.'

He sees their longevity as a testament to the capacity of the CIEP's strong design and graphic architecture to endure within many different sites and contexts: 'It's an easy building to be integrated,' he says. Washington Fajardo attributes the vitality of the schools' facade and structure to the original choice of concrete as a primary material.

Lesson Five: Personal And Social Education

'As much as one might want to think of a monolithic curriculum, uniform for everyone, that's just not possible,' observed Laurinda Barbosa and Carmen Rangel at the Darcy Ribeiro Foundation. 'We used to joke that not even General de Gaulle could make all the school-children in France sing "La Marseillaise" every Friday morning.' Although standardisation was a fixture of each prefabricated school building, the original CIEP programme supported an innovative school curriculum that celebrated the unique social and cultural heritage of individual sites. For instance, every CIEP featured a group of 'cultural animators'—local people who introduced regional dance, music and other popular cultural and artistic expressions to the school.

We encountered cultural animation first-hand during our visit to the *CIEP Doutor Antoine Magarinos Torres Filho*, located in the heart of the Borel favela. As we sat inside the bright blue octagonal library building, we met samba teacher Francisco, a.k.a. 'Chiquinho', who was setting up percussion instruments minutes before a class of children were due to arrive from the main teaching block.

As we learn from the director Lenita Vilela, a large samba school is located across the road from this CIEP. Every day its vibrant, musical rehearsals can be heard throughout the neighbourhood. Because samba is such an integral part of the local community and cultural identity, Vilela felt compelled to add percussion classes to the curriculum. 'The kids demanded it', she joked. On our heels as we left the library moments later, the infectious rhythmic beats resounded through the air, filling the school's open spaces.

According to Jair Valera, the samba school itself was originally intended to be something like a super-CIEP. When it opened, the *Sambódromo* was the largest CIEP of all—a school with a potential intake of 15,000 pupils. Classrooms were to be located under the bleachers and the large processional route acted as a playground—but government funding was cut just a few years after the experiment began. Today the Sambódromo still hosts the world's most famous and spectacular carnival celebrations, but its days as a pioneering large-scale school have passed by long ago.

Lesson 6: Politics

At the imposing *Rio de Janeiro City Hall*, we met with Claudia Costin, Secretary of Education for Rio de Janeiro (now Senior Director of Education at the World Bank), and Rafael Parente, under-secretary of New Educational Technologies, who reflected on the evolution of the CIEPs. When Costin first arrived in the state, she remembered how unfashionable CIEPs had become. 'It was as if it had been a mistake. And I don't believe they were a mistake,' she said. 'I was very sad when I saw the way the CIEPs were becoming ruined—nobody was cutting the grass, for example. They were not painted, they were not taken care of… ' Major aspects of the original programme had been discontinued, including Ribeiro's cornerstone idea of full-time education. However, their neglect was not due to failure. The discontinuation of CIEPs was largely political. '(The CIEPs) became a trademark of one politician', Costin explained. 'Everybody wanted to disassociate from Brizola, and so there was an aversion to the buildings themselves.' Successive governments with markedly different political priorities consequently withdrew funding and support for the CIEPs.

In retrospect, Jair Valera also believes that it was a mistake for the project to be viewed as a political statement, tied to one political personality, ideology and party: 'CIEPs became known as *Brizolãos*… It was hard for later governments to support the project, as success would be seen as a validation of Brizola's socialist ideology. Therefore they withdrew support and underfunded, some say sabotaged, the project.'

Today in Rio, the CIEPs are receiving new coats of paint, the grass is freshly cut, and Claudia Costin does not subscribe to the same stance taken by her political predecessors. Instead, she recognises the CIEPs as 'part of an important moment in the history of Rio, when there was this heavy investment in education it was a time when they thought that poor kids should have a better chance. You don't kill the project just because some people thought Brizola was a populist.' She continued, 'Even if in the beginning it was slightly naive, we have to recapture this naivety—the good side of this naivety. The idea that it's possible to change the lives of these kids. If we don't believe in this, then why have public schools?'

This text was originally written on the occasion of Aberrant Architecture's first research trips made to Rio de Janeiro, in spring 2012. Since then several details have changed; notably, Oscar Niemeyer passed away in December of the same year.

CIEP Nação Rubro Negra, here viewed from the road, is located near Ipanema Beach, in the city's largely affluent Leblon neighbourhood

Schools That Are (like) Wings
    Ligia Nobre

May 2016: It is almost three years since the outbreak of civil demonstrations in June 2013 in Brazilian cities. Today we are experiencing significant turbulence across political, economic and social spheres, spread across the country. Just at this moment, one of the most meaningful movements is the occupation of state schools by their students, most of whom originate from lower income groups. First arising in São Paulo at the end of 2015, school occupations continue to multiply throughout Brazil today, across the states of Rio de Janeiro, Goiás, Alagoas and Ceará. Education emerges as a fundamental political agenda, this time through the actions and voices of adolescents themselves. Students are demonstrating for their demands: a quality public education service, accounting for the difficult conditions they face, including issues of housing and urban transportation; against the scrapping and precarity of public schools; against the scandal of corruption in the provision of school meals; against censorship of teachers and for freedom of expression. Violently repressed by an authoritarian State, acting through the military police, these high-school kids and their protests in schools—as well as in the streets, public spaces and legislative assemblies—have invented other forms of existence and resistance, both learning and teaching us a new politics of friendship and collective agency, through the contested narratives and forces at play.

In this complex context, it is impossible to ignore echoes of the CIEPs—examined in the research project described in this book—which continue to resonate through the fields of politics, education and architecture in Brazil, and particularly in the urban environments of São Paulo and Rio de Janeiro. Following the exhibition of *Animating Architecture: Learning from Rio de Janeiro*, as part of the Venice Takeaway at the Venice Biennale and in London, the project by *Aberrant Architecture* was included in the X Architecture Biennial of São Paulo in 2013, within the exhibition *Modos de Ser Moderno (Ways of Being Modern)* at the University Center Maria Antonia—University of São Paulo. The work was subsequently acquired by the Museu de Arte do Rio (MAR) in the city of Rio de Janeiro, as part of its permanent collection. Indeed, it was part of an exhibition at the MAR in 2014—which proposed, "models to think about the potential of education"— which took as its title a quotation from the Brazilian educator Rubem Alves, still so current and poignant for the student-led occupations across Brazil today: 'There are schools that are cages and there are schools that are wings.'

The *Integrated Centers for Public Education* or CIEPs were the greatest utopian attempt of the acclaimed anthropologist, educator and writer Darcy Ribeiro. Implemented across the state of Rio de Janeiro, during the two-term governance of Leonel Brizola (1983–1987 and 1991–1994), the CIEPs would become the urban embodiment of the ideas and practices formed at the *Park School* of Salvador in Bahia (1947–1951), ideas initiated by the educator and thinker Anísio Teixeira (d.1971), who had called for a 'universal, public and free school.' A key mentor throughout the life and career of Darcy Ribeiro, Teixeira was one of the pioneers of the *Escola Nova* (or New School; Teixeira contributed to a manifesto of the same name, published in 1932), primarily responsible for introducing the ideas of the North American, John Dewey (d.1952) to Brazil, thus laying the foundations for educational democratisation in the 1930s. The first trial of the Integrated Center concept was in Salvador, gathering various academic classes within a 'school park', in a bid to provide full-time access to education for children from poor neighbourhoods. This was part of an educational project for a country strongly marked by the inequality of access between social classes.

The expansion of the space given to school sites precipitated several large school-building projects in Brazil: the *Park School* in Salvador by the architects Helio Duarte and Diogenes Rebouças, for example, or later in Brasilia by the architect José Reis. The CIEPs by Oscar Niemeyer in Rio de Janeiro in the 1980s led to the development of the CIACs *(Centro Integrado de Apoio à Criança, later renamed Centro de Atenção Integral à Criança or Comprehensive Care Centres for Children)* by the architect José Filgueiras Lima (Lelé), adopted at a Federal level in the 1990s. The *Centros de Educação Unificada*—CEUs or Unified Education Centers—were built in São Paulo by the Department of Buildings of the São Paulo municipality, during the 2000s. Echoing their educational philosophy, the architectural features and composition of school blocks attempted to use scales and insertions that would seem compatible to their territories, integrated with local communities and cities, and symbolically representing the intervention of the State within the urban landscape.

Entitled *Cidade: Modos de Fazer, Modos de Usar* or City: Ways of Making, Ways of Using, the *X São Paulo Architecture Biennial* proposed and reflected on dialogic modes to make and use the city, between 1960 and today. This platform also resonated with the politicised agendas emerging during the events of June 2013, such as urban transportation and occupation of public spaces. Curated by Guilherme Wisnik, Ana Luiza Nobre and myself, this collective research was developed in close dialogue with collaborators and partners, bringing together a total of 180 projects, including exhibitions, film screenings, seminars, workshops, talks, music shows, performances, residencies and urban interventions throughout the city.

The exhibition *Modos de Ser Moderno (Ways of Being Modern)* posed the question of how to re-evaluate our Modernist legacy, as well as paying simple tribute to the iconic architect Oscar Niemeyer, who died in December 2012. In the triangulation of projects presented, the interest was in the activation and articulation of two archives, within which recent political issues—particularly urban and educational issues in Brazil—remained latent. Firstly, the *Arquivo Brasilia* (2010), product of much research and careful restoration of early photos depicting the construction of Brasilia (and satellite towns), together with current photographs made by artists Michael Wessely and Lina Kim. This project was complemented by *Animating Architecture: Learning from Rio de Janeiro* (2012), created by *Aberrant Architecture*, a research project with 508 models of CIEPs across the city and state of Rio de Janeiro. Pictures of Brasilia spread like a fan along a long curved wall, while the models of CIEPs were compounded into a large cube of overlapping blocks, solid and airtight. Here was Brasilia: the new political capital of the country, and here, Rio de Janeiro: the old political capital, and a city that seems set, in a way, to recover its protagonist status through global sporting events. Both Brasilia and the CIEPs are ambitious projects, with significant scales of production and territory. Both make heavy use of reinforced concrete, a main and strategic technology in the country's process of self-development. Both were built through rapid and short-term programmes: the new capital was inaugurated in 1960, a few years before the military coup of the subsequent dictatorship (1964), while the CIEPs in the 1980s fell at the beginning of Brazil's period of re-democratisation. And of course both were designed and built with the participation of Oscar Niemeyer, his teams and partners, along with thinkers and politicians who aspired to build a nation.

By investigating the CIEPs programme in Rio de Janeiro and highlighting its features and unprecedented strengths—the use of standardised architectural design of high quality, open to their contexts, implemented on a large scale in poorer areas of cities, originally linked to the ideas driving a nascent democracy—*Animating Architecture* contributed to an updated discourse on the political dimensions of education and architecture, both in Brazil and England. If architecture and the state had experienced endemic relations since the 1930s in Brazil, then in recent decades large infrastructural projects—often laced with marketing-speak and other shady processes—seem to be implicated in massive corruption between contractors and politicians, criss-crossed by the flows of global capital. Conversely, the political dimensions of education and educational dimensions of politics are as strongly present as they ever were. Sparking demonstrations in the streets, in student movements, in our bodies and in minority actions, knowledge—and the empowerment it brings—is shared and multiplied, in an attempt to release new perspectives, grow new wings.

Ligia Nobre is a São Paulo-based architect, researcher and curator, working through experimental projects and collaborative platforms between art and architecture. Her practice has travelled across international locations from Nairobi to New York; she is also part of the artists collective O Grupo Inteiro (with Carol Tonetti, Cláudio Bueno and Vitor Cesar). In 2013, Ligia was one of the co-curators of the X São Paulo Architecture Biennale, and of the exhibition Cidade: Modos de fazer, Modos de usar (City: Ways of Doing, Ways of Using).

Learning by Numbers:
Distribution of CIEPs across the State of Rio de Janeiro

01 Rio de Janeiro ×134	13 Resende ×6	25 Piraí ×2
02 Nova Iguaçu ×87	14 Petrópolis ×6	26 Santo Antônio de Pádua ×2
03 Duque de Caxias ×45	15 Nova Friburgo ×5	27 Valença ×2
04 São Gonçalo ×44	16 Barra do Piraí ×5	28 Araruama ×2
05 São Joâo de Meriti ×27	17 São Pedro d'Aldeia ×4	29 São João da Barra ×2
06 Campos ×16	18 Teresópolis ×4	30 Cabo Frio ×2
07 Niterói ×10	19 Três Rios ×4	31 Casimiro de Abreu ×2
08 Volta Redonda ×9	20 Macaé ×4	32 São Fidelis ×2
09 Magé ×8	21 Paracambi ×3	33 Vassouras ×2
10 Itaboraí ×7	22 Angra dos Reis ×3	34 Cachoeira de Macacu ×2
11 Itaguaí ×7	23 Itaperuna ×3	35 Maricá ×1
12 Barra Mansa ×6	24 Nilópolis ×3	

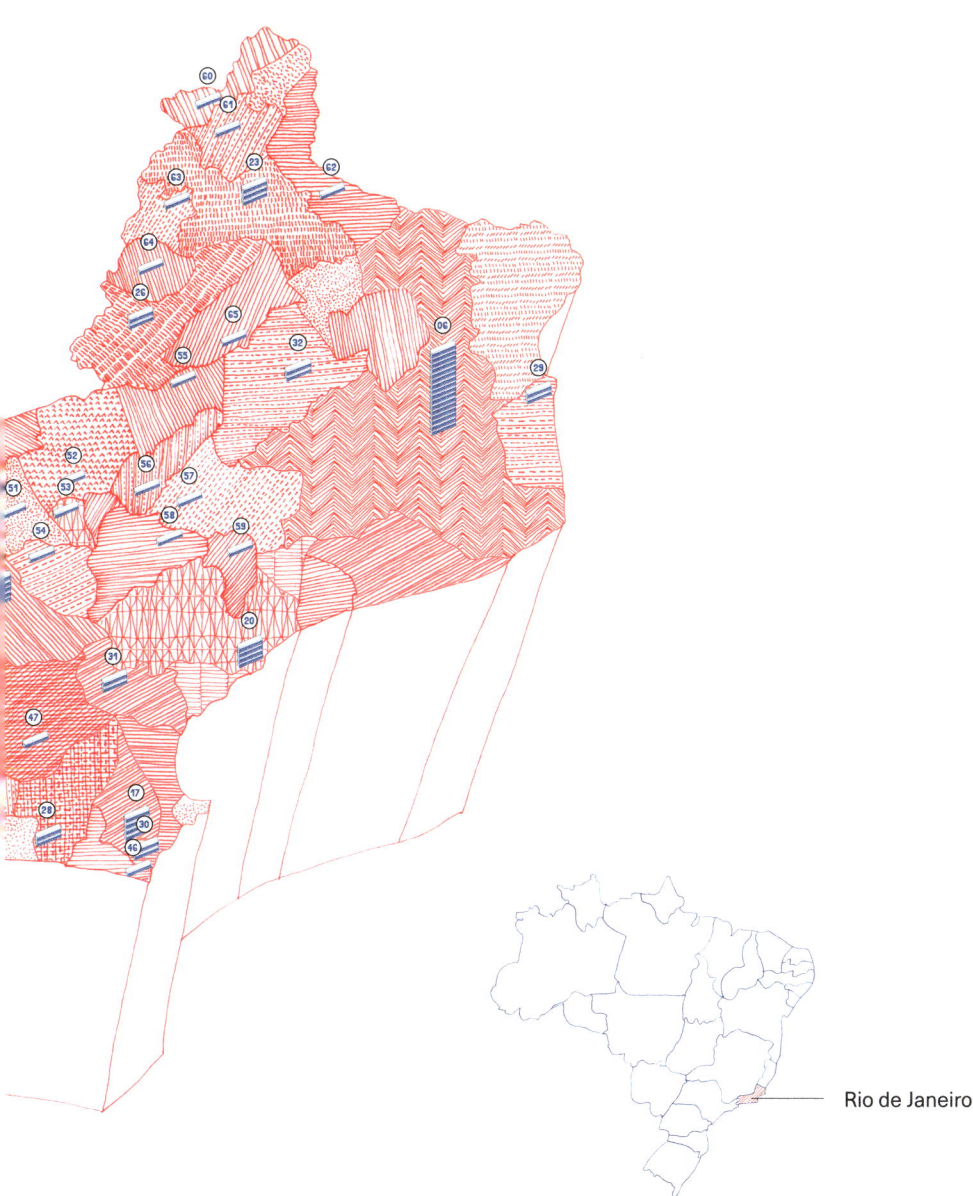

Rio de Janeiro

36 Parati ×1	48 Sapucaia ×1	60 Porciúncula ×1
37 Rio Claro ×1	49 Carmo ×1	61 Natividade ×1
38 Mangaratiba ×1	50 Sumidouro ×1	62 Bom Jesus de Itabapoana ×1
39 Rio da Flores ×1	51 Duas Barras ×1	63 Laje do Muriaé ×1
40 Paraíba do Sul ×1	52 Cantagalo ×1	64 Miracemi ×1
41 Mendes ×1	53 Cordeiro ×1	65 Cambuci ×1
42 Paulo de Frontin ×1	54 Bom Jardim ×1	66 Pati do Alferes ×1
43 Miguel Pereira ×1	55 Itaocara ×1	
44 Saquarema ×1	56 São Sebastião do Alto ×1	
45 Rio Bonito ×1	57 Santa Maria Madelena ×1	
46 Arraial do Cabo ×1	58 Trajano de Morais ×1	
47 Silva Jardim ×1	59 Conceição de Macabu ×1	

The book plays an important role as an educating agent; CIEPs libraries are open both to the school and to the wider community

Why Build Public Schools?
    Shumi Bose

A school stands in a busy metropolitan neighbourhood, announcing itself with an unconventional and imposing form, enlivened all over by children boisterously sprinting, sliding, weaving, gliding through it. Not long has passed since its architect died, and the design bears a signature style: swathes of smooth concrete, a dynamic sort of weightiness, and virtuoso engineering. In a country that has hitherto been extremely hostile, this is the architect's first school building. The area is notorious for drug-related crime rates, social deprivation and racial tensions, so the presence of such a powerful building means a lot to the local community; a point of pride for the neighbourhood, giving importance to, and placing faith in, the future of its youth.

The school in question is not one of the CIEPs, and the architect is not *Oscar Niemeyer*. This is a very different building that manifests the concerns of its own time: the *Evelyn Grace Academy* by *Zaha Hadid Architects* in Brixton, London, to which we will shortly return. As the places where our children learn how to negotiate the wider world, school buildings often reflect the social and moral climates that produce them. It follows that radical societal programmes can take their shape in and through the architecture intended to educate our future generations. When such programmes are supported by the State, we can suppose that school buildings may truly embody our attitudes—towards ourselves, each other and our broader realities.

The examples so lovingly and critically examined in this book speak to this aspiration: the CIEPs programme of *Leonel Brizola*, *Darcy Ribeiro* and of course Niemeyer represents a serendipitous moment of synchronicity in technological, social and political will, synthesising an architecture of enduring ambition. Rio's CIEPs schools were defined by the dual contexts of Brazil's new-found democracy and an admirably fertile collaborative spirit, but as we try to learn from them, we should note that such has it ever been; there are parallel points in both British and Brazilian schools which express the social values of their time, as expressed through their design. Let us take our lessons from history:

Built in 1969 (and demolished in 2008), the *Pimlico School* was a weird experiment in British brutalism; a real love-or-hate dealbreaker. For starters, the Pimlico School embedded itself in a pit, sinking below the street. Rising from the same subterranean level as the basements of the neighbouring Georgian-stuccoed houses, it physically ingratiated itself with the local community from the literal 'bottom' up. Rather than distancing itself behind fences or a playground, it extended itself as a fluid territory; the school's interlinked levels, projectile cantilevers and controlled views allowed for privacy whilst maintaining a visual access with the schools' urban context. For the local municipality and for local parents and students, here was a different way of thinking and talking about education and its place in society—at least initially. Designed by *John Bancroft*, a largely unsung municipal architect, Pimlico School was by far his best known and most notorious project, drawing much professional attention at the time. But as well as exercising Bancroft's individual flair, Pimlico's provocative design reflected the ambitions of the 1960s: to use the latest technology—including self-cleaning canted glass windows and innovative concrete casting—to create an egalitarian and open society; a 'well-tempered social environment'.

Travelling further back in time, a decade before Pimlico and a few years after the end of the Second World War, another notable state-funded school was commissioned by Norfolk County Council. *Alison and Peter Smithson's* design for *Hunstanton School* (completed in 1956; the architects were 21 and 26, respectively, when they won the commission) is widely regarded as a physical manifesto, of what was dubbed by the critic Reyner Banham as the *'New Brutalism'*. If Brutalism—coming from béton brut—described a certain massing of raw, unfinished concrete, then New Brutalism espoused, in arithmetic terms, the idea of 'showing one's working'. The building is legible, didactic and uncompromising, revealing its austere material palette, the clarity of its layout and context. Undoubtedly controversial, some heralded it as the future of school building, while others found it too harsh: the steel structural frame, welded on-site, is plainly visible and redolent of an industrial heritage; advocating the use of 'as-found' components, relatively cheap standard sections are used everywhere, while inside all the finishes and pipes are exposed.

Hunstanton was the first state-funded building to show the architecture of necessity as an ideology, in the manner often alluded to by *Mies van der Rohe* (whose texts were a touchstone for the Smithsons). But in contrast to Pimlico—demolished in front of a baleful Bancroft, and replaced by an irredeemably poor one on just half the site area —this building has been recognised for its architectural significance, is now listed and well-loved. Showing a growing acceptance of Modernism, it was brave—in the desperate optimism of Britain's post-war recovery—for a regional council to build for such a polemic architectural statement, and for the Smithsons to decide that the proper vehicle of that polemic should be a school.

Both Pimlico and Hunstanton are remarkable outcomes of state-funded radical architecture, intended for public use. Confusingly, 'public schools' in Britain are not the same as 'public sector' schools, as the former term describes expensive, fee-paying establishments. *Eton College*, Britain's most famous 'public' school is an example par excellence of this contrarian nomenclature. Emerging from the religious-led charity schools of late Medievalism, Eton was founded to educated 70 'poor' children; it has since educated generations of aristocracy, including 19 prime ministers.

Indeed the history of British school-building did not involve the state until the nineteenth century. The intellectual salons held in the homes of the elite tell us something about elite enclaves of knowledge, as restricted sources of soft power. Further back, the church and other charitable groups led the building of schools: their mission was largely philanthropic, producing a compromise between the idiom of what was seen as right for church architecture, and the philanthropic institutionalism of strict moral fibre. Take the sandstone Quaker schools, which interpret an ecclesiastical vernacular at a humble and domestic scale, or the noble neo-gothic redbricks of the Victorian era. This moralising attitude extended to building programmes: Liverpool's *Blue Coats* was one of many schools that took upon itself the responsibility of housing its students, and living quarters were intended to distance the students from their impoverished parents, who were seen as a bad influence.

Innovation in public sector architecture peaked after the Second World War, when technological optimism was met with the moral fortitude and political agenda to rebuild Britain as a modern, progressive society. Here was the birth of the *National Health Service*, of generous social housing programmes, and the faith that design experimentation would ensure that the prejudices of the past would never again strangle the hopes of the future.

With the exception of a millennial florescence in iconic cultural projects—like so many baubles on a globalised Christmas tree—governments today require stringent justification for civic building programmes, and are generally averse to bold architectural propositions. Zaha Hadid's Evelyn Grace Academy, unlike the 508 CIEPs, was a one-off; impossible to replicate, the school is managed by private hedge-fund *ARK* (Absolute

Return for Kids), who seek to apply the neoliberal terminology of entrepreneurialism to the lives of children. Unlike the CIEPs vision to integrate the school within mutually supportive societies—and entirely in keeping with the stultifying diktats of today's market-led reality—the Academy building supports local urban regeneration; the processes of speculative, inegalitarian venture capitalism are ennobled in the firm's 'parametric' design.

Incidentally, Zaha Hadid Architects' office operates from a Victorian school building, one of hundreds built to the standardised designs of Edward Robson following the Elementary Education Act of 1870, which introduced universal free education across England. Such schools became beacons of dignity in areas where there was little; today, their enduring spatial qualities makes them desirable as converted flats, start-up offices or design studios. In evaluating the legacy of the CIEPs programme, as with the climatic failures and material audacity of the Pimlico or Hunstanton schools, the intention of this book is not to gauge a performative success or failure—but rather to examine the values therein, which carry through to broader society. Though separated by time and space, the CIEPs of Brizola, Ribeiro and Niemeyer, built in to the fabric of Rio de Janeiro, inspire its authors and hopefully its readers with the potential of humanistic ideas, championed by pioneering design and a supportive state.

Shumi Bose works across diverse platforms in architectural and cultural production. She teaches architectural history and theory at the Architectural Association, the Bartlett School of Architecture at UCL and is a Senior Lecturer at Central Saint Martins. Shumi has co-edited several architectural titles including Real Estates: Life Without Debt and Common Ground: A Critical Reader; in 2016, she was co-curator of Home Economics, for the British Pavilion at the 15th Venice Biennale of Architecture.

One of the brightly coloured classrooms designed by Aberrant Architecture at the Rosemary Works School in London's De Beauvoir Town

Inventing Other Stories
>A Conversation with David Chambers & Kevin Haley

During the final stages of producing this book, Kevin Haley and David Chambers, co-founders of *Aberrant Architecture*—took a time-out with writer and curator Shumi Bose, to reflect on their own school memories, observational design processes and the widening remit of architecture.

>**Tell me about the schools that you went to, as children.**

KH It's been a long time since anyone has asked me about that! It was St Thomas More Roman Catholic School in Walderslade, Kent.

DC I went to Clydach Infants and Junior School, near Swansea in South Wales. After a while, my mother—she's a teacher, so she was really mindful about education—decided to move us to Ynystawe Primary School, in the next village.

>**Can you remember anything significant about the actual buildings that you studied in?**

KH Well, St Thomas More RC was also the local church—I mean the school was located in the same set of buildings. So we would go to school, every Sunday, for family mass! Actually, the church was open at the weekend for lots of things: fétes, markets, competition days, picnics… There was always a reason to be there. I don't think that's very common.

DC There is one thing I remember, architecturally. My school was one of those old red-brick buildings; it had a colonnade, with covered arches—like the CIEPs, actually! But the place that stands out in my memory is the local art gallery, which ran arts and craft classes. I remember making things in ceramic, and winning a drawing competition there when I was five. I think that kind of introduction to the arts stays with you; it's a great thing to experience. The CIEPs tried to address the fact that a large segment of society, for various reasons, is unable to access those things.

>**Having thought about your own childhood experiences, what do you think children get from being in Niemeyer's iconic buildings?**

DC Well, let's talk about that question for a minute. The physical environment on its own doesn't do anything; you need the curriculum to activate the space. This idea that architecture is mostly focussed on the building itself—more than anything, I think the CIEPs are *not* about that. They're about an understanding of spatial practice where design works hand-in-hand with the programme: the needs of curriculum and community are combined with the built form.
So to sit here now and separate out the physical object… We can talk about it, but it's important to clarify that the way the CIEPs were used by the community, all that stuff was intrinsically fused with the building design from the beginning. I think that's why we find the CIEPs interesting as a project, because we believe that architecture as a profession is much wider than the production of physical forms.

KH Even early moments in the process—like the Mendes meeting—implied, right from the start of the process, that the CIEPs would be produced by a big team of people coming together. That really sums it up, the act of reaching out to the entire educational community and debating ideas to get their input.

DC Another important point, which became clearer as we re-examined these interviews: the CIEPs, as the intended project, existed for just seven years, seven years only. So it's very hard for us to talk about it: what it is right now, is not what it was supposed to be.

Today, we might describe the CIEPs project as a very 'top-down' process—and it was, with only teachers and so-called élites planning the way forward. But the idea of 'bottom up' didn't really exist, especially not in Brazil in the early 1980s. Coming out of the military dictatorship in early 80s, and building a radical school programme intended for a community in which many parents can't read or write—it was hard to find ways to allow for a meaningful contribution.

> **What about now—is it always right to involve as many actors as possible with a project like this?**

KH   Not always. There are false 'participatory' processes, which use this sort of narrative of participation to make it feel or appear like they are more inclusive.

DC   We both have a real belief in process; our best projects usually come out of a natural process, involving lots of different strands. But sometimes that process can be short-circuited, or rushed, and that kind of insincere consultation can actually become damaging to the project.

> **What do you do in your own work to make sure that participatory efforts are not superficial?**

KH   We would never begin with a preconceived outcome or a fixed idea of what we want to do. I'll give you an example from Liverpool, where we made the *Social Playground*. We were drawing with a group of local senior citizens, to help them express ideas of architectural identity. This old fellow, John; he just looked at me and said, 'If you want to know what it's like to live in Liverpool, we're going down the pub.' So I went to the pub and had three pints with him, and I learned much more by listening to him with an open mind. I think it's about staying flexible and being prepared to adjust, in order to achieve the most sincere results.

> **Let's talk about your practice; you call yourself a think-tank as well as a design studio…**

KH   That is to emphasise the fact that we are research-driven in our design process, because I don't think that all firms are. Most of our projects start through a process of research and enquiry—perhaps into historical precedents, or emerging issues in contemporary lifestyles. We try to pose questions, which we then like to share and explore. Our design process continues to test those questions in physical space.

> **Why don't you pick a couple of your early projects and tell me how you found your feet.**

KH   The studio launched in 2010, and the early work arose from our student projects…

DC   We've always been excited by understanding the everyday—by how people actually live, work and play in their everyday lives. I would definitely say that our backgrounds play a part in this tendency towards the 'normal'. We inevitably bring our own experiences to our practice. Our work tends to resist elitist, hyper-intellectual tendencies in architecture—good design doesn't have to resort to being obscure.

KH   Even our decision to draw comic strips that explain our projects: why do we do that? We do it because we want to get feedback not only from critics of architecture, but from people outside of the discipline. And some of our research is from experiencing and observing ordinary life. I remember once, we were laughing about an advice column in a magazine on working from home, and the strains it can place on personal relationships. A couple of years later, we examined the same subject during our residency at the *Victoria and Albert Museum*, questioning whether home-working was an architectural problem or a much bigger, societal one. In hindsight, that silly magazine column spawned several topically-related projects—*Gordon Wu*, *Devil Amongst the Tailors*, *El Paso* and the *Gopher Hole*—in our early career.

DC   The *Gopher Hole*, with the curator Beatrice Galilee, is one project that stands out for me. The premise was to investigate architectural discourse in the realms of popular culture. So we created an event-space that was completely removed from the academic world of architecture. That set a tone.

>   **I think it was fundamental that you situated the Gopher Hole event-space—intended to expand architectural discourse—in the basement of a public bar, the El Paso.**

DC   Exactly. Situated in the community, the bar or pub is a place for the everyman, for everyone. Victorian pubs often had a community room where local people might hold civic meetings, forming societies and networks. So we lifted this idea for our *El Paso* project—a community space where different people could come and meet, all nestled underneath a Mexican-themed co-working space and bar!

>   **In Brazil, Niemeyer, Costa and others found huge opportunities to build through state-led architectural programmes. In the UK, we experienced the same thing during the sixties and seventies. But as young architects, the form of practice you have chosen has led to various outcomes, which do not yet include a building.**

DC   Well, we would love to make buildings, of course!

KH   But even given the opportunity, we would have still done the Gopher Hole. I don't think it's one or the other; being an architect is not just about making a building. The Gopher Hole demonstrates how our prior research on the Victorian pub led to a real test of a spatial idea. These days, young architects wouldn't be trusted with big decisions for the city or the state; that responsibility might be too much of a risk. But an ambition for this practice is to at least be involved in those conversations.

DC   The stage of research and testing through smaller projects, it's a very important learning curve. We would really love to build, but you can learn a lot through doing the things we do well.

>   **Is that learning curve—of smaller, mostly public projects—also part of a decision to engage a broader audience?**

KH   Yes, for sure. When we started out as a practice, we wrote a manifesto—as young architects will do. I remember we wrote, 'We care more about people than we do about iconic buildings.' We didn't begin with the idea of making buildings; it was more to do with connecting to what's going on around us, people, life…

DC   We like projects that have a slightly wider cultural remit. To be honest, we're still just starting in that sense—but projects like the *Tiny Travelling Theatre* or the *Roaming Market* all attempt to deal with the everyday, with street life. Both the Tiny Travelling Theatre or the Roaming Market work by allowing moments of spontaneous interaction in the street—which has increasingly become our leisure space. They talk about the increased importance of the street or public realm, as a place of communality and coming together. I don't think this shared agenda between all of our projects was necessarily conscious, but there are patterns.

>   **So thinking about the social or public focus of your works, do you think design appreciation is a universal instinct, is it something intuitive?**

DC   We sometimes refer to design in 'layers'. We always try to provide something immediate, let's say on the superficial 'image' level. The more you engage—either visually, in the conceptual narrative or the process of how something has been made, the more you'll find to enjoy. For example, with the *Tiny Travelling Theatre*, people can engage on a visual level, but they might find its effects on the street, or the historical narrative to be interesting too.

KH   The point is that there are different ways of appreciating design, there isn't just one way to understand a piece of work. For our designs at the Rosemary Works school, we studied Edwardian architectural interiors and historic strategies for organising wall territories and nooks. When we asked the children about the spaces they wanted, they started drawing similar, individual little spaces for themselves. So then we could go back and say, 'Hey, those things you were drawing actually have a special, historical relationship to this building!' And then people really begin to enjoy the narrative, they can find a real sense of value.

> Let's come back to the CIEPs. I'm putting you, honourably, in the position of Niemeyer. From his point of view, was there much drive to engage with the users?

DC   No. But again, at the time, the thinking was different... There are two things to bear in mind, and they both have a kind of relevance today. Firstly, the speed of the project: the CIEPs had to be conceived and delivered in an incredibly short time.

> So decisions had to be made quickly, right?

DC   Right: they only had four years. Of course, after four years Brizola's party lost the election, the project got put on ice, schools were left unfinished. Only when the same party was voted in again for another term, in 1991, could they finish the CIEPs project. Going back to Niemeyer: it is well known that Niemeyer was a card-carrying member of the Communist Party. But this is the only truly socially-minded project that he did. This was a common criticism made against Niemeyer: he called himself a Communist but he never made any social housing—his projects usually involve large-scale, formally impressive, iconic buildings. According to Niemeyer himself, he decided that he would only make 'social' projects under a credible government—otherwise his work risked becoming a hypocritical sop to the working classes. In that sense, the CIEPs project was incredibly important in Niemeyer's canon, because it was the only time that he was linked with a political endeavour that he truly believed in—that combination of the right politicians, the right architects—the right team to enact massive social change.

> We have spent some time discussing how the building is not necessarily the most important thing. But in the end, it is. The CIEP is a strong form, and there are strong figurative and formal traits in the work of Aberrant. Although concerned with the everyday, your work is certainly not generic.

KH   Yes, that's true. Personally, I think the CIEP is as iconic as some of Niemeyer's other works; when you look at the photographs, they stand out very graphically. But it's not the most important thing about the project.

DC   Niemeyer understood that if you're going to build a series of schools—intended as the new centres for the whole community—then they need to be prominent, they need to have an identity that stands out, that everyone can see, that is emblematic of a project that provides all these services and social spaces as well as a high-quality education...

> So did this project have a big impact on how you think about standardisation?

KH   Definitely. In my experience, the idea of standardisation and producing something repetitively—particularly in architecture—is often considered quite negatively in this country. When we first discussed the CIEPs project, I remember that I was really 'anti' the idea of standardisation as an approach to architecture.
But with the CIEPs, it's what you find when you look deeper into the project—the scale and the ambition of it, you know? The idea of involving a whole team of people rather than one single architect; providing children with 24-hour education; battling inequality

in cities… They're not so apparent, but those are the things that started to change my opinion about standardisation—mainly because when I looked at the CIEPs, it was clearly the appropriate strategy for the bigger philosophy. It becomes hugely relevant when you've got four years to change the lives of thousands of people.

DC   Actually, I've always been interested in standardisation. My undergraduate thesis was about temporary Roman military camps, which were among the earliest examples of standardised architecture. They started off with the same moat, the same guard towers; tents would be laid out in the same pattern. But over time, each camp would evolve in different ways. Later on in university, I got into structuralism, and the ideas of Herman Hertzberger—the theory of an architectural language that can adapt and inflect based on the use of space. I guess our visit to the CIEPs was the first time that I had seen that as tested and built.

KH   I really like that premise, of standardisation as a platform for personality. The infrastructure is provided, but then the designer steps back and the space evolves over time, through use and the people.

DC   It was just so ambitious, so audacious and so generous. 508 identical buildings, arranged in slightly different ways… And it's fascinating to revisit the CIEPs years later, to see how they have evolved. Some are successful, some less so, some of them are unused and abandoned. Their uses might change even more over the next thirty years, they could become other things. But what's interesting about the buildings—in terms of the architectural language—is their flexibility versus a kind of robustness. The CIEPs model was designed with local climate and expertise in mind: it's concrete, it's robust, it's resistant. Even though the project was criminally neglected by subsequent governments, the buildings are in good shape.

> **They are, and as you say, the individual adaptations and multiple uses make it a really vital or 'living' space. Which of the CIEPs' physical environments impressed you the most?**

KH   For me, it's the covered arcade, and the areas that are not just for the children but are open to the community, to people who are not even involved with the school. Dave was telling me that people have even had weddings there—that's brilliant!

> **Yes, it's the way that the buildings foreground education—not as something elitist that separates me from you, but as explicitly open to the whole community.**

DC   I completely agree with that. I also found the little residences on the roof to be fascinating. The 'common' spaces of the schools are so big, almost civic in terms of scale: the covered arcade, the sports court, even the ramps and the classrooms. But when you get onto the roof at the CIEPs that have the little houses, the scale change is really amazing—like little modernist cottages on the roof of a big ship.

> **It's true. I was thinking about that in terms of the CIEPs buildings—as schools they must be quite intimidating, they are vast.**

DC   They're certainly big, deliberately big. Remember the context: a lot of the children are living in the favelas, in dark, cramped spaces and informal neighbourhoods. So at the CIEPs—and this was a deliberate move from Niemeyer, to provide spaces where kids could run around freely—they experience a sense of light and space.

> **What does that say to you, in terms of the role of the school?**

DC   It's quite nice that the school can be read as a kind of public house. Not only a place for learning, but a place with a civic and even a domestic function. The issues that necessitate the residences on the roof are ultimately negative—they are for children who don't have a stable home life.

It's important to provide safe, intimate, relatable spaces. But in the little houses, you do feel like you're in your own little world, set apart from the big communal spaces. I think that combination of the civic and large-scale with the small and intimate is really powerful.

Several projects have seen you working in far-flung or unfamiliar places, like Gwangju or Hong Kong. What knowledge did you 'take away' from the CIEPs?

DC   We had not been especially concerned with educational spaces before researching the CIEPs. That interest has subsequently manifested in our interventions at *Rosemary Works Primary School*—a small, private school in London, where we have been conducting a phased series of refurbishments. When we first started designing at Rosemary Works, the clients had commissioned us to address one small part of the school. But immediately, we felt that in order to be meaningful we needed to do more than decorate a couple of classrooms. So the conversation developed into the idea of a programme of works to be delivered over a number of years.

KH   We evolved that idea by creating a set of standards or design rules, which the school could follow in future when making improvements. Since our involvement, the school has independently completed the refurbishment of more rooms, following the rules that we devised.

DC   Before the CIEPs project, a lot of our work looked into the idea of public realm, and how we could increase opportunities for social interaction—such as the *Tiny Travelling Theatre*, the *Roaming Market* and so on. Also the *El Paso* bar and the *Gopher Hole*—they share this intention of providing different kinds of social spaces. As a research project, the CIEPs provided a realisation that the same concern can exist within the typology of a school. Also, seeing the school as a place where multiple things can happen. This idea was very strong in the CIEPs: the school is part of the community and the community is part of the school.

KH   Initially, we were excited about this space outside the Rosemary Works school by the adjoining canal, where the staff would go and have a cigarette break. We made a little sketch to suggest what might happen if you opened this space up, put in a landscape of steps, made it into a community garden, allowed everyone around you to come and use the space... In the case of the CIEPs, the school is intended as the centre of the community, whereas here in the UK, the high street is still seen as the centre for most. That's a big shift, potentially.

DC   Yes. The CIEPs had a programme where the teaching in school was supplemented by local professionals and cultural animators who taught other skills, practical or artistic skills. This is something which, as Kev says, we're trying to explore—to see if we could use that outdoor space as a way of starting to invite the community into the school.

We were talking earlier about Niemeyer and the big gestural projects that he made. One of the most admirable and distinctive things about the CIEPs programme was the inclusion of Niemeyer alongside Brizola and Ribeiro, right at the beginning of this political and social project. Could you speak to that aspect of the programme?

KH   The thing to learn from the CIEPs is the linking of concerns. Practical synergy of those concerns—political, social and architectural—doesn't happen too often. In the case of the CIEPs, it was about assembling a broadly-skilled team of professionals and starting the conversation together.

DC   The whole project was this three-headed thing, led by the governor Brizola, the academic Ribeiro, and the architect Niemeyer. So even though the project had severe constraints of time, of budget, the same kind of constraints that we have today, the architect was involved at the top. Today, the architect's role has been attacked or diminished from all sides. The bulk of a normal building project is designed from the spreadsheet—that is to say, from cost and viability concerns. So your role as an architectural designer risks being reduced to façadism, or drawing a slightly different kind of box.

Interestingly, the CIEPs project was driven by similar pressures; they needed to build the maximum number of units in a very short time frame and within a tight budget. I'm speculating now, but perhaps one of the reasons why the CIEPs project turned out as well as it did was the near-mythical presence and status of the architect. Niemeyer was probably the sort of strong personality who, even within those constraints, could maintain an integrity of design.

There are large gaps in the process of making architecture from which architects are normally excluded. It is the developer who will create with the brief, the development model and the spreadsheets which prescribe the 'performance' of the building. Design is included as just another part of that spreadsheet.

> **Do you think there's a shift, or a resistance which might see the role of the architect expanding or changing? And do you actually think individual architects should get involved at ideological or political levels?**

DC   Yes! Well, some people would probably argue that the architect's role is purely to design the spaces; everything else is off the remit, right? Funnily, Niemeyer is often admired by those architects who profess not to link design with politics. He was definitely one of Zaha Hadid's favourite architects, for his sculptural form-making. But the CIEPs project was one case where, for Niemeyer...

> **His politics were on the line, right?**

DC   His politics were on the line, and he saw that potential.

KH   If you look at a lot of the young practices starting up today, it's obvious that the role is changing, isn't it? Because they're not just interested in producing aesthetics, if that's what you want to call it. They're interested in collaborative practice, participation, policy, writing, all these sorts of things. Perhaps the term 'architect' doesn't fully represent what the practice really involves today—particularly for those who are starting out in this new terrain.

Chapter 2
Fazimentos: Those Who Did

An aerial view of a CIEP outside the City of Rio de Janeiro; Niemeyer's design has a strong visual impact in various contexts

Not enough schools, over-crowded classrooms, a scarcity of funds and a growing gulf between private and public institutions. These are just a sample of problems blighting education in the state of Rio de Janeiro during the early 1980s. Brazil itself was at a major turning point, marking the end of military dictatorship and transition to democracy; for the first time in decades, free elections were held for governors. In Rio state, mass migration had swelled the urban population, but the public schools were unprepared to educate the growing low-income student body.

Leonel Brizola, Rio's newly elected state governor, responded to the crisis with the Centros Integrados de Educação Pública, or CIEPs: an ambitious school building project, dreamed up with the collaboration of respected anthropologist Darcy Ribeiro and visionary architect Oscar Niemeyer. The CIEPs constituted a radical change in the strategy for educating children from the lowest strata of society, offering an alternative educational programme.

Traditional public schools had focused on the provision of core subjects like numeracy and literacy, and only ran for part of the day. While this worked well enough for the fraction of children from Rio's urban middle classes—whose parents might have had the resources to provide cultural and extra-curricular activities—it wasn't enough for the disadvantaged majority of students, who had no access to anything of this kind.

Avoiding large bureaucratic structures, the CIEPs project was managed by a Coordinating Committee of Education (Comissão Coordenadora de Educação) a small, cohesive group that could instigate rapid, but massive change. This group mapped out the main objectives of the Special Programme of Education (Programa Especial de Educação); the CIEPs project was part of this larger plan. Crucially, the CIEPs purpose and goals were widely debated with teachers—in 1982 a pivotal congress was held in the town of Mendes to establish a common set of beliefs for the project.

The CIEPs' half-height walls were intended to create a feeling of openness; though some have been filled in, here they are used as display areas

Leonel de Moura Brizola (d.2004) was a statesman and politician, and one of the most radical, divisive left-wing figures in modern Brazilian politics. Brizola served as a state governor both before and after the country's military dictatorship: first as governor of his home state of Rio Grande Do Sul in 1958, and later twice in Rio de Janeiro (1983–1987 and 1991–1994).

Brizola was the first elected state governor of Rio de Janeiro after the end of military rule. Freshly returned from exile, his victory was a surprise to some but he appealed to a popular demand for profound social and economic change.

Brizola was a passionate advocate of public education: in his own experience, the provision of public schooling had enabled Brizola to lift himself and his family from poverty, becoming an engineer and later a politician. Previously in Rio Grande Do Sul, his belief in public education had motivated Brizola to commission 6000 smaller schools. In Rio de Janeiro, this ambition eventually paved the way for the CIEPs programme of school building and educational reform.

The Politician Speaks
> Leonel Brizola, The State Governor

The CIEP is a new institution that emerges from a process of questioning, from within, our unjust, inhuman and unpatriotic social reality. These new schools will provide our children with complete nutrition, academic classes, extra-curricular support that the poor have never received, sport, leisure, school supplies, medical and dental assistance. After spending the whole day at school, the children return, washed and dressed, to the care of their families.

Over 50% of our children leave school, after years of failure, barely being able to sign their names. In other words, they leave illiterate and resentful. Why? Lacking healthcare and nourishment, they only remain a few hours in the school environment, which, in turn, has been precarious and ineffective. The CIEPs' students, on the other hand, have received close to 90% in approval ratings. This high level of efficiency alone, even economically, justifies the Integrated Centres of Public Education.

Some might say that they should resemble the schools we've always had. Firmly, we say no. Our children deserve even more. They represent the most valuable part of Brazil, and also our own destiny as a free and democratic nation, committed to building a worthy existence for all its sons and daughters. Every child in this country should be in a school like the CIEPs. For this to happen, it would be enough not to deviate so many public resources for useless and unmentionable purposes. If we didn't pay the interest relating to our foreign debts for a period of two years, for example, all Brazilian children could be studying in a CIEP.

This short publication aims to bring a quick explanation of the realisations of our Government in the educational field to a greater public attention. Professor Darcy Ribeiro was my henchman. If not for him, his team of teachers and the whole faculty of public educators, we would not have been able to accomplish these important improvements, which crucially must be continued. We have built 500 CIEPs. The next Government must build another 500, or even more.

From the CIEPs men and women will emerge and go on to achieve, for the Brazilian people as well as for Brazil, everything we could not nor had enough courage to do.

> Rio de Janeiro, October 1986.

Originally published in 'O Livro Dos Cieps', (Bloch Editores S.A, 1986), a book intended to act as a manual for the CIEPs initiative.

Laurinda de Miranda Barbosa has held directoral and coordinating positions in the Secreteriat of Education for the City of Rio de Janeiro between 1983–1986, and in the State of Rio's Extraordinary Special Programmes between 1992–1994, establishing the Special Programmes for Education. She is Technical Advisor at Fundação Darcy Ribeiro (Darcy Ribeiro Foundation).

Carmen Maria Rangel is a teacher and coordinator for Educational Projects at Fundação Darcy Ribeiro. In 1983 she was an advisor at the Education Secretariat of the City of Rio de Janeiro. During the second Special Programme of Education, she led the Directorate General of the CIEPs programme.

A taxi ride through the winding streets of Santa Teresa brought us to the calm, elevated surroundings of the Fundação Darcy Ribeiro, overlooking the late summer haze of downtown Rio. During our visit on Wednesday April 4th, 2012, both Laurinda and Carmen were enthusiastic to share their immense experiences, from the earliest ambitions of Darcy Ribeiro, Niemeyer and Brizola—including the seminal teachers' meeting in Mendes—to the current challenges faced by teachers, students and communities on the ground.

A Conversation with Laurinda Barbosa and Carmen Rangel
	The Coordinators

LB	Look, I brought you some publications that the Darcy Ribeiro Foundation produces. This is Darcy, here *(indicating photograph)*. They are called 'Fazimentos'— which is actually a neologism, as this word doesn't really exist. Darcy used the word 'fazimento' to refer to himself, as a 'doing' or 'making' man, which means a man who *did*. So each year until the last one, the Foundation published something about the people who collaborated in the type of things that Darcy 'did', or about Darcy himself. This one is about Darcy himself and also Tatiana Memória, who was the Foundation's president for the first ten years.
	For so long?
LB	Oh, very much so. She was both the president and Darcy's confidant in the first instance, I mean, the closest person to him during the first two terms. *(indicating photograph)* This person here is Berta Ribeiro, Darcy's wife. She was an anthropologist and of course his partner for many years. Berta's archive file also belongs to the Darcy Ribeiro Foundation. She was a very important anthropologist in Brazil, producing some fantastic studies on indigenous Brazilian natives, one of the first people to do so: in short, she is a prominent figure.
Well, so here is one 'Fazimento' publication which refers to the Special Educational Program, the CIEPs… But it mostly talks about the Mendes meeting. Mendes is a city in Rio state, where Brizola—well, I'll wait until we get started, shall I! *(laughter)*
	Well, you must know so much… To begin with: when thinking of the original CIEPs project, what immediately comes to mind?
LB	Let's see… What I understand of the project is that this was the first time that Brazilian public education was considered with all the seriousness that it requires.
	Really?
LB	Absolutely. Because—I must give you a bit of history—when Brizola returned to Brazil from exile, right, and started talking about his return to politics, his attempt to regain the original PTB *(Partido Trabalhista Brasileiro, the Brazilian Workers' Party)* was based around a strong rhetoric on the importance of public education.
Brazilian public education was going through a crisis—especially in the large urban centres—because as a nation, Brazil was reversing an historical situation. Previously the country had a large population living in rural areas and a smaller population in the cities. With all the economic reforms, we began to witness a shift—a new population shift following the rural exodus to the cities, so that the number of people arriving in cities surpassed the number of those who remained in the field.
	So you are suggesting that the city needed to build more schools quickly, to serve these new people?
LB	What happened was this: the existing public schools were prepared for the existing urban population. The remit of these schools was the education of a new class: an urban, industrial labour force. They were really not prepared, even destabilised by the arrival of a rural population, one which had completely different skills… A population with a background in agriculture, raising livestock and so on, which now tried to settle in large cities like Rio de Janeiro, São Paulo or Belo Horizonte. So what happened? Public schools became unresponsive to a diverse population with varied cultural values, needs, skills—a different worldview, which was what happened when the rural population came to the city. So that propelled a crisis in education: public schools began to see high rates of failure and dropouts, because they could not meet the new social conditions.

So the existing schools were providing skills for what? For the service sector or more city-based jobs?

LB   To work in more urban industries, exactly. Getúlio Vargas and all those pioneers of education identified this idea in public education, you know? The aspiration was to enable a middle and lower-middle class urban population ascend to positions within the industries, whether as a manager, or in administration. The public schools attended to this need. Then came the rural exodus, and things got out of balance, right?

So that was it. Various Brazilian educators began to report this crisis. The CIEPs idea of a full-time school, with integrated curriculum planning, was proposed precisely to meet this situation, to overcome the crisis and enable a greater level of social inclusion.

Well, Brizola was elected governor of the State of Rio de Janeiro in 1982—to the general surprise of most people, as the competition was really between the two established parties. Brizola entered the scene and addressed a population that really wanted profound change, not least because this was the moment just after the fall of the military dictatorship. We were precisely in the transition between the military dictatorship and 'full' democracy, in quotes.

What specifically was Brizola's role in the CIEPs project?

LB   Public education was without doubt a major concern of Brizola's political platform. Hence the membership of the teachers' unions and so on, the Brazilian intellectuals, especially in Rio de Janeiro, were all favourable to him. Later that changed, but at that moment, there was widespread support. But what did you ask me? Oh yes. Previously, as the governor of Rio Grande do Sul (1959–1963), Brizola had already addressed the issue of public education, launching various state programmes. Under his leadership, some six thousand small schools were produced…

Six thousand?!

LB   Yes, it is a significant number, right? And in his own life, Brizola had a strong relationship with the idea of state education: his mother was a poor widow and he had the opportunity to become first an engineer and then a politician, all thanks to public schooling.

Well, when he became the Governor of the State of Rio de Janeiro, he brought this idea or concern to the foreground, together with Darcy Ribeiro who supported him as the Vice-Governor. Darcy's appointment demonstrated the concern for education, as he too had a history of educational reform in Brazil. In fact, the CIEPs idea was actually proposed by Darcy Ribeiro, he came up with the scale of it. He convinced Brizola that now was not the time to make small schools but rather large schools, with a programme that allowed children to stay in school full time.

How big were the smaller schools?

LB   They had something like five or six classrooms. They were really small. But why push for big schools? Well, this was an idea for a school with another perspective, one where the child stays in school all day. A great school, equipped with a kitchen and dining room, eighteen diverse classrooms and a dedicated room for crafts, to work with their hands. Each of the CIEPs had a big outdoor hall with a sports court and bleachers for watching the games. Do you understand? They even had the possibility to have rooms with television, they could watch television with teachers to discuss and reflect on the new language that television brought…

On the issue of size, were there a thousand children in each CIEP?

LB   Yes, six hundred students during the daytime; in the evening the CIEPs operated something called Young People's Education, for people between 14 and 21 years old. That programme accommodated up to four hundred students in the evening.

So, six hundred students in full-time school education from 7am to 5pm, and four hundred young people from 6pm to 10pm.

So one thousand students over the course of the whole day.

LB   A thousand students. Well, that was the proposal. So what does Darcy do: he constructs 12 theses which outline his ideas on education, ok? He builds these ideas along with a team, he doesn't build it alone. Yes, he formed a team and then called Maria Yedda Linhares—a collaborator of his since the opening of the *University of Brasília*. So, as I said, Darcy already had a lot of ideas about education. He had studied the North American John Dewey, who preached pragmatism in education and about the importance of handicrafts. He had read Claparède and others authors in France... All of these were absorbed into Darcy's idea for a new kind of school.

The 12 theses were distributed to all public schools across the whole state of Rio de Janeiro—that is, around 2,500 schools in total. These theses or essays were discussed by the teachers in each school. And then representatives from Darcy's team would visit the schools, participating in the discussions, advising teachers with their methods and taking part in the general debate of schools.

It is important to keep in mind that at this point, we were in an important transitional period between military dictatorship and democracy. Each school elected teachers to represent them as delegates and then Darcy invited them to discuss their thoughts with him. The school delegates got together for a meeting in Mendes, a town around 90km from Rio de Janeiro.

And when was this, what date?

LB   This was in 1982. This document recounts the testimony of attendees. Their discussions, Darcy's theses, it is all here *(shows 'Fazimento' document)*. So in Mendes there were some very important debates between teachers, some of whom stood out at the time, discussing new ideas like the school curriculum running full time instead of in half-day shifts, as it previously had been...

The real work started after Mendes. With the approval of the school delegates around the state, Darcy could push for real action. And that's how the Special Education Programme began.

That's fascinating. Looking back, I think what is really interesting about the programme was the actual process of 'designing' it. One question on that, actually: it seems to involve the teachers and the educators, but was anyone speaking to the communities directly? Did anyone ask them what they thought about their requirements from the schools?

LB   Not at that moment, no. The Mendes debates didn't really include that aspect. The issue of community participation and discussion is a bit more recent; it didn't exist at that time, at least in Brazil. But during the physical construction of the CIEPs, there were people debating these issues with the community. I myself went to visit many places to ask whether this type of school would work for this or that community. A school that serves children or teenagers, you know? We started to discuss these things with the communities during the actual construction of CIEPs, but not before that. And I say 'we', even then—I was part of Darcy's team or secretariat at that point, and it was collaborative as far as possible, which is why I am saying 'we'.

It sounds like the community was involved only once the CIEPs schools were being built. But if you would do it again, do you think that you would involve the communities earlier in the actual design of the programme, or even the buildings? Or do you think that actually, it would not really be worth it, to do so?

LB   No doubt, no doubt, no doubt. Almost 30 years later, I have no doubt that it would be an important thing to include. But that is how it was done at the time. The idea was really to create a new idea of a public school that really attended to the poorest sections of the population; one which aimed to provide a better, more complete education, more appropriate for children from poorer backgrounds.

This is interesting—and I'll sound like I am saying bad things about my country—but normal public schools, where teachers were prepared to teach middle-class boys and girls, had a sort of constituted model of a typical student—even if he or she was not from the 'rich' middle-class, but middle-class. This, then, was the generic model child which formed the basis for planning public school education.

But very often, when children from poorer communities would attend these schools, they would not correspond to the perceived model—coming from a very different background and living condition, and lacking extensive cultural stimuli, do you understand? They might not have had any of the cultural stimuli that a middle-class child would have—they would not have the books, the television, the experience of travel, visits to the theatre or cinema, none of that.

The CIEPs provided a very different spatial environment too, not least in terms of their size. Interestingly, we observed that the children would run through the schools; the environments in which they lived were often composed of very small, cramped or dark spaces. So then beyond the basic literacy classes, the conditions of light, the space, the sheer freedom of movement that the school offered... *(breaks off)* Carmen, come here and join us, I have already started!

CR   Nice to meet you!

And you!

LB   I was just at the beginning, it's a good moment to join us. I had just got through the context of the Mendes debates and so on, and was starting to talk about the schools themselves.

CR   And being politically incorrect, no doubt, ha ha ha!

LB   Ha ha ha. Well, the idea was that children from poor families had this new opportunity to stimulate his or her ability, intelligence, cognitive thinking; their feelings towards aesthetics, ethics, everything—it addressed this view of the whole person. And accordingly, there was a strong policy of teacher training.

I would like to ask how much influence Darcy Ribeiro had on the architectural aspect of the project.

LB   Carmen, you can talk about this.

CR   Yes, I can. I mean, Darcy Ribeiro worked closely with Oscar Niemeyer in this conception of a pedagogical space that had some level of integration with the community. The sites were chosen that way—people would say, 'Oh, the CIEPs are outdoors by highways', but this is not true. Some are based near roads, where we had available sites. But some are embedded right within the communities, especially in the city of Rio de Janeiro, where that sort of location would be of greater impact for disadvantaged populations.

Did that come from Darcy?

CR   This was his concern; indeed this was the concern of the state government itself, which aimed to place the CIEPs schools as closely and accessibly as possible to the communities where children and young people actually lived.

Ok. And did Niemeyer have any input into the curriculum?

CR   Well, if we consider that the architecture was especially designed for such an educational project, it is clear that there is a relationship. For example, when Niemeyer

Front entrance (top) and internal ramps (bottom) linking the three floors of CIEP Doutor Antoine Magarinos Torres Filho, in Rio's Borel district

proposes the half-walls in CIEPs, he does so with a clear goal. He used to say: 'Teachers must learn to speak more quietly and children too.' So, the sound interference, he said, 'would only be minimised through a process of self-education, for both teachers and students.' In that sense, the architecture had everything to do with the education process inside the CIEPs. Another thing about the half-walls; they allowed for the classrooms to be cross-ventilated and therefore always supplied with fresh air. These half-walls were their idea, Darcy's and Niemeyer's, but I'm not sure which one of them came up with each idea in every case. Another great feature is the ramps. Today, Brazilian schools must have disabled access. But to include the ramp, 21 years ago…

LB   21 years? No, it is more—almost 30!

CR   1982–1983, Right?

LB   Almost 30 years!

CR   Well, they already suggest a building that allows access for anyone, be they walkers or in a wheelchair. So, it is already very advanced. And I think another interesting thing about the architecture is the CIEPs ground-level space, which has one large 'canteen' space in a corner—a covered part that could serve as a refectory, a playground and so on. At the opposite end, they acted as medical and dental centres, in the sense that one of the pillars of the education programme was health.

LB   A thousand things were possible in that space!

CR   There is another thing to mention. When space was available, or where the site was big enough, the CIEPs' design included a large covered gymnasium, with stands for onlookers. This was designed for various activities and practices, but it was intended to be more than just a courtyard—in the absence of any other municipal provision, it was a space for exercise and audience gatherings. Some of the CIEPs built during the second term of the Brizola government even had swimming pools.

There were also the libraries, again in the absence of any other similar service; where the CIEPs site could accommodate it, these libraries or reading rooms were constructed as separate modules. Above the main buildings were communal houses for some of the children, which we called 'Social Residences'. That was also part of the educational programme, to take care of children who have difficulty living with their families during the week. They could live in the school—up to twelve boys and twelve girls, cared for by appointed 'social parents' in the residences. The social parents were very often firemen or police officers who were also living in the residence.

> **Why do you think it was so important for the reading room or the covered courtyard to be separate from the main building?**

CR   Oh, there were two reasons. Firstly, it was based on the size of the site; when there was no space on the site, the residences and libraries were on the top floor. I mean, I think it was more a composition within the site itself, than an architectural necessity…

> **So it was not an idea of allowing for a consciously separate destination that people—even people who were not students—could go to read or play sports, for example?**

CR   Not really, but it is true that in the CIEPs where the modules were separate, the community had more access.

LB   The community did have access, this is important. In many CIEPs, a secondary programme ran across the whole weekend with a schedule of activities, right? The library would be open, and the sports court… For students and their parents.

> **That makes sense. Can we talk a bit more about the curriculum? Each school was built to a standardised design, but it seems to be an attempt to use the curriculum to make each school specific to each location…**

Students enjoying the showers (top) after using the outdoor multipurpose room (bottom) at CIEP Presidente Tancredo Neves, in Catete

CR Okay. We might first understand the curriculum as an always-contested space, a space for discussion, I mean, for negotiating knowledge. But that this knowledge is consolidated—I mean, in the school culture of this country, knowledge is both consolidated and experienced differently by the students, by the children and young people that come to school. So clearly, the curriculum is always a space of negotiation. I mean, there is no other way, right? As much as one wants to think of a monolithic curriculum, uniform for everyone, there is no chance. We used to joke that not even General de Gaulle could make all the school-children in France sing 'La Marseillaise' every Friday morning! Yeah, so it is inevitable that changes do happen and will happen within the curriculum.

> **Maybe you could give examples of these changes or differences between schools and aspects of the curriculum... Or how the local cultures might have entered the different schools.**

CR Ah. Well, the biggest vehicle of this integration was the Cultural Animation platform. Yes. You see, the curriculum was delivered and elaborated through 'work projects'. These projects brought together teachers, health professionals and cultural professionals. I will give you a simple example about head lice.

LB Oh yeah, the lice!

CR There were a lot of lice outbreaks at school. While the classroom teachers discussed personal hygiene matters, there was also the question of diseases that can spread... So health issues were discussed by teachers at schools, and the other professionals involved in the work projects would help to plan these lessons. From bodily hygiene, the need to wash your hair, to clean your nails, to wear clean uniforms, and so on, and how these things had health implications. The work project teams would write poems, texts, songs... They interviewed nurses, doctors... The cultural animation platform was an effort to understand how such matters were culturally represented in these communities—how such communities view and understand issues like scabies or fevers, to see how the schools could build upon the things they already believed. There were all sort of strange customs: people who would use their own recipes, like putting olive oil on the hair, which made the hair oily and actually better for lice. There were even people using home-made toothpaste on lice! The work projects created a recipe made with grated coconut soap and other easily available products, following information from the health department. So the animation platform was created to show how the community might address such issues in their own way, understanding what is really effective and what is not. Toothpaste is not made to put on the scalp—it hurts! So, the work projects and the cultural animation platform was an integrated programme, for example bringing scientific knowledge from healthcare professionals team to be delivered by classroom teachers; at the same time it had to create a dialogue space with local cultural practices, in this case to get rid of lice. This is a classic example.

LB Yes, very well remembered.

> **I guess it is helped by using a method that students and parents could relate to... As they were used to these kinds of homegrown treatments, the problem is discussed in a way that they understand.**

CR Another thing: they were afraid of dentists. In general, the dental issue is very serious in Brazil, and this is no different in the poorest sections of the population. We would see seven year old kids entering the school with rotten milk teeth, and when they would fall out, already-damaged permanent teeth. So this matter of dental care was much discussed.

LB The food, all meals were balanced. And there was the water issue too.

CR   Yes, the water issue. The project was always reinforcing the idea that the more cleanliness there is in the place where you live, you know, the more hygiene you practice on your own body, the more protected you are.

LB   There is a picture here of a child taking a bath, you see? This was joyful. For many of the children, this was their first contact with a proper shower.

Really? That's incredible…

CR   Because baths were normally taken at home with a bucket and a can, right?

LB   It's very bright, but yeah, this is it *(shows picture)*. Look, here is the sports area that Carmen mentioned before, with the stands below. Can you see?

CR   And here, behind here there were showers. The girls learned to prepare their own homemade shampoos, taught by the health team and teachers. Reading the recipes was one of the lessons too: reading recipes in general, sometimes even in the form of poems, so healthcare and literacy were combined. The shampoos were very much appreciated—they really washed their heads!

So you mean they were made into poems in a style from their community, that sort of thing? As a percentage, how much of the overall curriculum was standardised, and how much was culturally adapted?

CR   You see, although in 1971 Brazilians were still living in a dictatorial regime, the Brazilian Ministry of Education had never established a standard and singular curriculum for the whole country after 1964. In 1964, the first law and policy was created, which formed the basis of national education; this already suggested that the curriculum should incorporate the experiences of schools and their students. As the former Minister Paulo Renato used to say, the common or shared content, which was more or less uniform, is set by the authors of the textbooks rather than any policy.

LB   Ha ha ha!

CR   Then, there was always the possibility of adapting the curriculum contents as necessary, especially in terms of Portuguese language issues—children and young people are in school to learn to read and write in the best way possible, right? Of course, there were some basic grammar lessons, teaching the rules and so on. And one should develop logical and mathematical thinking skills too, right? With these two great tools, students would be able to progress in whatever they want to study. But this learning had to be done with the help of the students' own experiences.
The other day, I used the example of physics class, where Luís Carlos Menezes, a teacher from USP, was teaching his students about resistance: power, conductivity and so on, right? Now, I don't know physics, I am just quoting him. So he said: 'Man does not discover things through formulas alone. He did not discover electricity through writing formula of resistance.'

LB   True, true, that's right.

CR   'Man discovered electricity through experiencing what it is—for example, by seeing how it could be used to conducted an engine. So this is the path that we can use to teach our students.' He would then go further: 'So, for example, I have devices that are resistors, right, like motor-operated equipment. If I want to compare the level of resistance, I could take a shower for example, or use an electric iron. Then I can start observing the difference in resistive capacity between things that work differently, for example, the blender motor and the shower, or the iron. What is the difference?' His intention was always to bring the familiar, real life experiences of the students into the classroom, so that he could theorise from there. I think this is a great method teachers should always pursue, rather than memorising formulas. So this dialogue develops by bringing what you know about something, together with the academic knowledge that must be present in the classrooms. But how to make this dialogue effective? This is why there was so much importance placed on the teachers and their training.

It sounds like quite a practical approach. Was there already an idea of the kinds of routes which students would follow after leaving the CIEPs? I mean, was there an idea that they'd go to high school and then go to university? Or certain kinds of jobs, what was the aspiration?

CR No, there was nothing intended. The Brazilian education system doesn't normally consider this. The Brazilian education has never had a system that demarcated that certain people would go to university and some people would not go to university. This is not France. In France, yes, you can see that clearly happening.

LB No, I've never seen it either. Not in Brazil.

CR There is another method of selection, but that is an economic issue.

Do you know of CIEPs graduates who've gone on successfully to university? Are there a lot of students who have done so?

CR Look, the project only lasted seven years. So at seven years old, a child could enter elementary education and leave at 14 years, go straight on to secondary education, and then to university. We did not experience much of that kind of continuity, unfortunately. Now, some research conducted at FAAP *(Fundação Armando Alvares Penteado)* shows us that some of the students who left after attending two or three years of school in CIEPs did indeed continue their studies in high school and finally went to the university. Now, we're seeing statistics of that.

LB There was not enough time…

CR Because the Brazilian elementary educational lasts for seven years and our project didn't quite last that long…

What changed?

LB Oh, political changes.

That leads on to the next question: the programme was always subject to change but what about now—how do they relate to the original vision?

CR Ah, today the project no longer exists…

LB No, nothing is the same, nothing.

CR Our desire—and Darcy's desire—was that it should continue the way it was, and in this way we have seen many advances. For example, we have children who had not managed to learn how to read and write in the public schools.

LB We still see this today.

CR … And we saw it clearly during the CIEPs programme. Kids came with huge difficulties, even the oldest children, twelve or thirteen years old. Because we have this problem in Brazil, right: the middle-class children start learning to read at two or three years old. But among the most deprived classes, children could spend six years at school without properly learning to read and write.
So we realised very well what a boost we gave them. The children came with huge difficulties, and they left properly writing, producing, writing pieces, writing poetry, writing letters…

So why did it stop, was it too expensive?

LB No, it was not.

CR The project required investment, of course. To support a child or young person to be at school full-time, with all the infrastructure needed—food, personal hygiene, uniform, books and materials, everything—this involves resources. Which Brazil does have, by the way.

LB   But on the other hand if students keep failing, this continued failure is also very expensive for Brazilian society, it is.

> Sure. But do you think that in a way the programme was dismantled as a reaction against Brizola and his government? Even that the new government might not have wanted it to be successful, because then it would reinforce support for Brizola and his positions…

CR   Yes, for sure. It's a deliberate discontinuity.

LB   That's exactly right. I am totally sure it is. Totally sure.

CR   The following government and all who followed that era—how could they possibly live with a school that people commonly called *Brizolão*?

LB   That's right—how could they live with a political project that really aimed access to the most deprived people, that aimed to give them a better living condition? It is very difficult.

CR   There is another issue that we can't ignore. I mean, the end of the second term of Brizola's government, brought neoliberalism to the Brazilian situation, right? So, this is in sharp contrast to Brizola and Darcy. Darcy was son of a teacher from the interior of Brazil. He always held this strong principle of education, it was very clear for him. While Brizola was a poor boy from a farm in Rio Grande do Sul, who had managed to change the course of his life only because he was able to go to school.

LB   Exactly. It is irreconcilable.

CR   So when he was governor of Rio Grande do Sul—which is a big state—Brizola built some six thousand small schools in the countryside, to tackle this issue of education. In 1965, less than 40% of the Brazilian children between seven and fourteen years old went to school. School was for a very few people. So I mean, people who think like that are usually replaced in government by people who analyse development through privatisation of public goods.

> Do you think that Darcy Ribeiro and Brizola were in a rush? Like, in a single four-year mandate, did they feel pressure to get the CIEPs programme done fast—perhaps that is why it was all modular?

LB   Oh yes, they must have felt this pressure very strongly. Brizola used to say: 'I am the Government, I am not the situation.' He was very clear on this point.

CR   Yes, he was swimming against the current and he knew it. When Darcy stated 'We will build five hundred schools,' everybody said, 'This is insane! Megalomaniac!' But he would only respond, 'But we need to build schools in this country! And we need five hundred of them in this state.'

LB   If they hadn't made five hundred, we wouldn't be here having this conversation today. Certainly not.

> Yes. And they must have known that there was a very good chance they wouldn't have finished in just four years. Would you say that this really influenced the architecture?

CR   Ah, for sure. Today, even if we don't have a full-time pedagogical project, we at least have the buildings. The schools exist. Brazilian education needs another programme of investment! Children must stay in school longer. There is more to learn! Take the emerging technologies in information and communication: increasingly, man produces more knowledge!

LB   And with each step, schools are realising that they must integrate with the community. This municipal government of Rio de Janeiro has said that by 2020, all municipal schools of the the state will be full-time.

CR   It is a goal.

LB   Which I do not believe… but it is a goal, it is a goal. That's how it must be perceived as today: there is an appeal from society.

CR   That period was a very interesting time. During the 1980s and 1990s, many people were against full time schooling: 'School is not a restaurant, school is not the doctor's office, school is not shelter, school is not this or that!'

Today, all the people who once criticised the CIEPs now consider full-time education as the only way forward. We used to have terrible encounters with the teachers' union on behalf of CIEPs. The CIEPs' teachers were working all day, so they naturally earned more, but we would hear, 'There are two categories of teacher: the hourly teacher who earns bad wages and CIEPs teacher who make two or three times more.' Today, the union makes time to debate the issues around full-time schooling.

LB   Yeah. I think we were the vanguard. Ha ha ha!

Yes, you were!

CR   I mean, nowadays in Brazil it is very clear that in order for people to learn, especially those people with less general cultural access, they need to be more exposed to content. School is the best place for this.

LB   Yeah, that's for sure. It is a democratic space, for access to knowledge.

CR   Especially because there are activities that young people and children only attend if they are promoted by the school. You know, like going to the theatre, cinema or cultural centres. Because they don't feel comfortable to go otherwise. Laurinda has a great story from when she was working at the Youth Education Department at *CIEP Lauradio*; she proposed a trip to the *Bank of Brazil Cultural Centre*. They asked, 'Teacher, which clothes do I have to use? Will I be allowed inside there?' If they could go inside, indeed. I mean, people are worried about the possible preconceptions.

LB   They were dazzled! 'Can we go there alone? Can we come back?'

CR   It is an important to note that these young people were not living in the countryside. They lived in the city and were used to seeing these places every day.

The CIEPs were built for a purpose, a vision that… A vision that is no longer in place…

LB   Exactly right. There is a local project called *Escolas do Amanhã (Schools of Tomorrow)* which includes 150 schools distributed across the municipality of Rio de Janeiro—several of them are CIEPs schools.

CR   Well, the CIEPs buildings, anyway.

LB   There is an intention in the municipality of Rio de Janeiro to extend the duration of the school day to seven hours. But the perspectives on education is another thing. You know, the thinking, the vision for life, the body of education itself is another thing, right.

CR   Yes, a teacher can perceive this very well. I mean, it is a more of a bureaucratic enterprise to manage the question of putting one million kids in school—any school—than a question of allocating each child to a school that is really able to help such people move forward in terms of education.

LB   There is a huge attempt to standardise. From the beginning, the intention of the CIEPs was not to make a parallel network to the existing public schools; they had a specific purpose.

CR   When you work in an NGO, the bureaucratic issue has to be handled very carefully. Otherwise you run the risk of burying the most radical parts of the project.

LB   Exactly.

CR   You run the risk of misrepresentation and failing to reach your goals, you run the risk of people feeling estranged in this process.

People have to be involved, you have to listen to their opinions—even when they aren't

users of this school, because they pay for it. Because in Brazil, public school is free of charge—but of course it isn't free, it is expensive as hell!
LB   Everyone is paying for this school!
CR   Right—I'm doing my income tax this very week. We all pay our income tax, though it is too expensive!
LB   It is absurd! What we pay is about as much as the value of a new car. But then there is a separation. The public schools are for poor people, so...
CR   They used to say: 'Public schools have problems', as if the private schools do not. Look, my son works in a private school, for upper middle class families and children. The monthly tuition fee, for part-time studies, costs around 1500 Brazilian Reais. The children at this school face problems of violence, abandonment, absent families, divorced parents—the same problems that any school sees—with one difference. These children pay a huge amount of money, so they must be carefully handled by the school. Public school is free of charge, so if something doesn't work out no one is responsible for the child's learning.

> Just one more question. Have you learned from any other international examples of educational programmes?

CR   Yes, I do believe that Europe also has some great lessons.
LB   In 2000, I visited France, through the Education Department, to attend a conference in Paris on the issues faced by French public schools. Now, the issues that were being discussed in Paris were well-known to us. The crises that schools passed through, especially those schools located in the poorest areas, they had very similar problems to ours in Brazil.
Did you see the film *'Entre les Murs' (The Class, 2008)*, about a French public school...
CR   Located in a very poor neighbourhood.
LB   That's right—a really poor population. Black, Asian, total diversity: they are all French citizens and all have the right to public school.
CR   Now, I think that the biggest lesson that Europeans need to take on is that these people have the right to be there. Because the Earth is for everyone, not just a few. Secondly, Europe developed itself through a project of colonisation, one which took the wealth of those countries that are now in need. They have a social debt to the rest of the world. This is the second issue that I think is important. The third is that every man is equal. Men and women are equal, there are no different people.
There's a great Brazilian thinker, a geographer called Milton Santos, who wrote a very interesting work called, 'For another globalisation'. Santos says that it is useless to think that people in remote areas will not participate in capitalism. They will participate in an incomplete or violent way.
LB   Exactly.
CR   Of course; they are so alive! They have to eat, they have to live, they have children and so on. Either they will participate in an incomplete form or a violent form. I think this is the biggest lesson, which we also need to learn—the middle class and elites must also learn. And in terms of lessons, or continuity: Brazil has two architectural project dedicated to full-time school designs: first, the CAICs which were built by the Federal Government. In the State of Rio, there are some but they are across the whole of Brazil.
LB   CAIC stands for *Centro de Assistência Integral Criança*, which is the Integrated Centre for Child Care, something like that. These were produced during the Collor government, by the architect João Filgueiras Lima.
CR   He is known as Lelé, his nickname was Lelé.
LB   That's right. Lelé was an architect who worked with Niemeyer, and also with

Darcy. Several schools have been built following the architectural designs and materials of Lelé. At Maré, the *Armando de Salles Oliveira* school is one of Lelé's projects.

CR   There is also the CEUs project in São Paulo *(Centros de Educação Unificados, or Unified Education Centres)* which were built under the governance of Marta Suplicy, from the leftist Workers' Party.

LB   That is a very interesting proposal, quite close to the CIEPs project

CR   They are even beautiful buildings…

LB   Really beautiful!

CR   The CIEPs project is really inspired by the great experience of Anísio Teixeira, who was really the founder of public education in Brazil.

LB   That's right! It was Anísio Teixeira that…

CR   In the 1920s, Anísio Teixeira went to study at the United States. He returned in a state of total enchantment. The United States at that moment was a thriving democracy, just before the 1929 crisis, the Great Depression.

LB   Exactly.

CR   He returned to Brazil with a liberal perspective, in which a good school was one that contributed to the maintenance of democracy. The liberals did share some common ground, in the end, with the more progressive parties.

It recurs again and again, this wave of concern around schools and education. School as a major site or space for the construction of knowledge, especially for those who have been crippled by the ongoing processes of this consumer society. The benefits of education and culture, most of all, would contribute to the consolidation of democracy. Anísio was a philosopher, an educator.

LB   He was the first to propose that children should attend school for longer.

CR   He created the Carneiro-Ribeiro Centre for Education *(Centro Educacional Carneiro-Ribeiro, or the Park School)* in Bahia.

LB   Yes! Here there was a space where children were given formal training in the morning and complementary education in the afternoon…

CR   He used to call this idea 'Classroom School' and 'Park School'.

LB   Anísio's ideas were more North American: the school that belongs to the community, managed by that community.

CR   Yes, that's it. They met when Darcy returned from studying the indigenous Brazilians. You see, the ministry for education is actually the Education and Culture Ministry; even today the acronym is MEC. Matters around Brazil's indigenous population and services towards their protection were managed by the Ministry of Education and Culture. At that time, the field of humanities, anthropology and social sciences —including the study of education—was really just in formation.

So Anísio and Darcy were in the process of creating, as they would say, an intelligence from their research in Brazil. They founded the Brazilian Centre for Educational Research *(Centro Brasileiro de Pesquisas Educacionais or CBPE)* in 1952. Because somehow the social sciences area was connected to education, and education was connected to social sciences.

LB   It is a part of social sciences.

CR   They met through trying to create the first platform for educational research in Brazil. Even today, the fully expanded name of the National Institute of Educational Studies is actually *Instituto Nacional de Estudos e Pesquisas Educacionais Anísio Teixeira*, or the Anísio Teixeira Institute.

LB   Additionally, Darcy was part of a Brazilian intellectual group which believed that research and scientific development was…

CR   The engine for evolution, for development.
LB   The engine for development, exactly. In Brazil, the question of development still remained.
CR   This generational moment that Laurinda is describing—Darcy was around eighteen or twenty years old, a student at the *Universidade de São Paulo* (University of São Paulo), still the largest Brazilian university today. He found himself among a remarkable generation of social scientists, historians, geographers and linguists produced at USP at that moment; there was a boom in the study of social and human sciences in Brazil. They had a non-intellectual attitude, very different from the academic who studies his object from a far distance. But they aligned their own perspectives to those of the reform movements that would eventually lead Brazil to development.
LB   Yes, exactly.
CR   Florestin Fernandes, Darcy Ribeiro…
LB   Celso Furtado…
CR   Celso Furtado, Caio Prado Júnior…
LB   Caio Prado Júnior, of course!
CR   Antônio Cândido, Josué de Castro, all these people…
LB   And they had a very interesting views, some of which are in danger of being lost, on Latin American issues.
CR   The issue of Latin America, 'Latinity' *(Latinidade)*
LB   Latinity. That was another characteristic 'issue' for this generation of Darcy's, it was important.
LB   If you let us, we will keep going… Ha ha ha!
CR   So that's it, really.
         Truly, thank you so much. Muito obrigado.
LB   It was really good for us too.

Chapter 3
A Fabric Of Schools

CIEP José Pedro Varela in Lapa: the pudding-shaped Catedral de São Sebastião is reflected in the glazed office block behind the school

Large, prominent and visually distinctive, the CIEP schools were widely and immediately popular. However they also drew criticism; some argued that such heavy expenditure would have been better used to renovate existing schools. Counter-arguments held that the introduction of high-quality buildings was necessary to 'dignify' those from poorer backgrounds, to overturn pre-existing stigmas. A radical new educational programme deserved a radical new architecture to support it.

The challenge was to produce beautiful, spacious buildings in a manner that was economically viable and rapid to construct. That challenge was entrusted to Oscar Niemeyer, whose precast concrete design delivered the CIEPs as a kit of parts, costing 30% less than conventional construction and deliverable in just a few months. A grand total of 508 CIEPs were built in towns, cities and favelas across the whole state of Rio de Janeiro—an area about double the size of Wales. The schools were described as a custom-made infrastructure, made to support a full-time integral education programme. Each CIEP was made of three main components: the school building (5,400 sqm), a multipurpose hall (1,080 sqm) and an octagonal library (320 sqm). Some CIEPs featured small 'houses' on the roof for live-in pupils; others even had an outdoor swimming pool.

Flexibility in the arrangement of these components was important, as finding sites to build all 508 schools proved difficult. Consequently, CIEPs are often found in unlikely but highly visible locations—along highways, in the middle of squares, or on elevated hillsides. Where it was not possible to accommodate all three components, a compact model was introduced in which the multipurpose hall was located on the roof of the main building.

Niemeyer's distinct design—with its rhythmic, lozenge shaped windows—has a strong graphic character, allowing the CIEPs to assert their unmistakable presence in urban and rural sites alike. As a result of their scale and repetition, the CIEPs have acquired an instantly recognisable identity.

Concept sketch for the CIEPs design, drawn by Oscar Niemeyer: the open hand and flowers of nature suggest an attitude of generosity

Oscar Ribeiro de Almeida Niemeyer Soares Filho (d.2012) was undoubtedly Brazil's most famous, cherished, enduring and award-winning architect, best known for the design of many iconic civic buildings in Brasília, the nation's first planned and capital city. Although he was influenced by Le Corbusier amongst others, particularly in his use of reinforced concrete, Niemeyer developed his own distinctly Brazilian, curvilinear expression.

An avowed communist, Niemeyer did not believe that architecture alone could change society. To him, that was the work of revolution, the citizen; wary of producing state-sponsored architecture as a political tool, he refused to engage until he felt able to support the government in question—happily, this was the case with Leonel Brizola. Despite their massive scale and replication, the CIEPs still bear the unmistakable hallmark of Niemeyer's designs. Niemeyer had already worked with Darcy Ribeiro on a university proposal for Algiers, which proposed educational spaces as a means to integrate the community. The CIEPs allowed Ribeiro and Niemeyer to develop their ideas in their home country and in partnership, realising what is arguably Niemeyer's only truly social project.

The Architect Speaks
        Oscar Niemeyer, The Architect

The criticism that has been being made about the CIEPs is so shallow, it shows such misapprehension that I'm unwillingly obliged to provide an explanation.

I'll begin by saying it is a revolutionary project, from an educational point of view. A school that not only seeks—like the old ones—to instruct its students, but also to provide an effective support to all the children of the neighbourhood. This explains the idea of a school that stays open for them during the weekend; of placing, on the ground floor, the gymnasium, a medical office, dentist, library, etc. From there comes the difficulty in using old school building—continually remodelled—as they have not been made for such a programme.

On the other hand, the CIEPs do not represent huge costs, nor can they said to be pharaonic (using a term that pleases the unavoidable mediocrity). They follow a standard programme and there is no magic in the field of their construction. Prefabricated, they constitute savings of 30% compared to a normal construction process—and they become even more economical considering the speed of their construction, approaching four months, and the ease with which one may control or augment the quantity of materials, manual labour, and so on. They can adapt to any site, even in the favelas, which is certainly important, allowing the children of the favelados to feel that every comfort is offered to them without that odious discrimination which, both later and for now, life imposes upon them. And they are simple, logical, their distinct shape causing them to stand out in various parts of the city, thus revealing the magnitude of the programme adopted by Governor Leonel Brizola, and which for this reason, does not seem to please many people.

But it's not just these easily explainable aspects that compel me to pen this little text. I am revolted, principally, by the ease with which some would comment on the educational programme of CIEPs without taking into account the presence of Darcy Ribeiro, an international authority in the field of education, constantly invited to develop teaching programmes in countries across the New and the Old Worlds alike. And this revulsion grows when I feel that most of these critics understand nothing of educational problems, being limited to opinions that are already well-established, easy to contest and define.

Now the campaign against the CIEPs grows when certain City Hall councillors, in order to align themselves with the more reactionary currents of this country, attempt to participate in the debate—as if they had nothing to tell people about their own programmes of governance. The Carioca watches all this with disillusion; as each CIEP arises, a new doubt appears, to counter those who insist on fighting against them.

Originally published in 'O Livro Dos Cieps', (Bloch Editores S.A, 1986), a book intended to act as a manual for the CIEPs initiative.

Washington Fajardo is an architect, urban planner and president of the Instituto Rio Patrimônio da Humanidade (Rio World Heritage Institute), a municipal agency responsible for cultural and historic aspects of the city. This concern has gained extra significance since Rio itself was awarded UNESCO World Heritage status in 2012. Fajardo joined the Rio City government in 2009, and is a special advisor to Mayor Eduardo Paes on various planning issues. Fajardo was the curator of Juntos (Together), for the Brazil Pavilion at the Venice Biennale of Architecture in 2016, which celebrated informal, activist housing and urbanism strategies. On Tuesday April 3rd, 2012, at the the Heritage offices in Laranjeiras, a busy Washington sketched out the architecture of a typical CIEP as he discussed their legacy and future evolution. His experience early on in his career, in specifically researching school designs, provided an overview of the CIEPs within a continuing series of state-supported school-building programmes, each with their own successes and failures. Furthermore, his opinions on heritage and preservation offered some reflection on the future of the CIEP buildings.

A Conversation with Washington Fajardo
> The Urban Planner

> **How much do you know about the original CIEPs project?**

WF Well, where to begin... I used to work in the refurbishment of schools in Nova Iguaçu, a suburb in the metropolitan area of Rio De Janeiro. The City Government at that moment wanted to start a huge programme looking at schools, so we studied historic cases and their architectural solutions. I started to study the CIEPs and the CEUs from São Paulo. Well, the CIEPs present an architectural image that is very well known to Cariocas, and for Brazilians in general: it's a quite strong graphic form and there are a lot of them. In every part of Rio de Janeiro you can find a CIEP, not just here in the city centre but also in the most interior part of the state. In small towns or beach places, Angra dos Reis, Praias—even in the most exotic or touristy places, there is a CIEP. So for Cariocas, the CIEPs are a strong image, in terms of what they stand for and what kind of solution they propose.

The architectural solution is impressive, because it allows schools to be fabricated in large quantities. In fact that was the name of the factory: the *Fábrica de Escolas* at President Vargas Avenue, where they produced prefabricated components.

In the 1980s I was not yet an architect, but I remember the construction of the schools very well. I used to live in a city in the interior of the state and I remember how impressive it was, it was very fast, the construction process. The architectural plans are very simple, even humble. There are arguments about the quality of the internal built environment. There are problems with noise, that's the most well known criticism of the CIEPs in an architectural sense. It came from a sort of Utopian idea that Niemeyer and Darcy Ribeiro had, to create a space without walls, but there are problems when it comes to giving classes in this kind of space.

But on balance, these buildings are amazing and still in really good shape, even now. You saw the Catete CIEP; if you come to Nova Iguaçu, in the furthest urban sprawl of the city, you will find more CIEPs in good shape too. Sometimes they are abandoned but the building is still fine because the structure is sound. For me this is a very important aspect of the architectural project to produce buildings on a massive scale—their condition now is some kind of proof that it was the right decision, as the schools are still in good shape and are well used.

> **How quickly could they be built? I mean, from the components leaving the factory to actually arriving on site and finally welcoming the first cohort of students?**

WF I think they could make a complete CIEP in six months. You have the basic building and then there is a series of associated buildings, and these produce different solutions on different plots. So as Catete is quite a narrow plot, you have the school building and the sports court placed in a line; in the *CIEP José Pedro Vargas* in Lapa, the arrangement of the school, the sports court and the library work very well because it's a modern building but it looks vernacular.

It was such an intelligent solution from Niemeyer, because it works so well in different kinds of places. It works in the city centre and in very small towns; it has a very strong urban image. There is no hierarchy: just this rectangle, always the same. And then the arcade, which works very well, especially when it appears on the street-facing side, creating a strong building frontage. They built more than 500 CIEPs just in the state of Rio alone, which is an impressive quantity. There are even CIEPs with swimming pools. And the building design also works in places where there is no city, just landscape.

Going back to the sites for the schools, how were these selected?

WF   They had a plan for the whole state. The sites were chosen wherever there were concentrations of people. I can't think of anywhere in the world—even though I don't know the whole of the world!—where you can travel across a whole state and find an identical school building, whether you're in a beach town, or on top of the mountains: wherever you find people, you can find the CIEPs.

It is amazing.

WF   Although I do think that in some areas, they might even have too many. Some of them are very close to each other. In Nova Iguaçu, you would sometimes find two or three of them in the same neighbourhood; I don't know exactly what brought so many together in such a small area. I think that it was very easy to build a CIEP, very quick, and the cost of producing them was very low too.

At first the CIEPs belonged only to the state government, whose educational policy was to promote full-time education. And now, we are again holding a lot of important discussions about how full-time education is important, strategically, for this country. That was the original idea of the CIEPs; they are not only good buildings, but buildings specifically made for this kind of full-time education. The kids could spend their whole day in this space; they were fed, showered and they also got medical care, even a dentist.

At this time in the 1980s, it is important to describe the political context. We were leaving the era of military dictatorship; the governor Leonel Brizola and the anthropologist Darcy Ribeiro, who were in political exile, had returned to Brazil after twenty years. Niemeyer was also exiled during the dictatorship, he lived in Paris and other places. Their education programme was, I think, one of the most powerful public policies in Brazil at this time. And I believe it is worth noting that the level of education in the state of Rio de Janeiro is higher than any of the other states.

Then or now?

WF   Now. I think it is interesting to see how they relate, the physical space and the educational programme. There are a lot of 'experts' who argue that the quality of learning spaces is not that important. They maintain the importance of full-time education, we need to provide that, but it seems, at least to some, that we don't need to change the space.

Do you agree, do you think that such a programme can be delivered anywhere?

WF   I don't know. Of course, I'm suspicious because I'm an architect. But space is important, always, and not only in terms of the visual or even physical realm – that is a very superficial concept of space. It's not only space in that sense but space as a kind of infrastructure. The CIEPs is in fact an infrastructure to support this ambitious educational programme; that was its real intelligence.

Can you think of any other examples of spaces or buildings that relate strongly to an educational programme?

WF   The City Hall of Rio de Janeiro actually has a long tradition in building public schools. As it used to be the nation's capital, the first public schools in the country were here. But more recently, São Paulo had another school-building programme called CEUs, which I mentioned earlier; it shared the same principle of prefabrication as the CIEPs but with a more complex architectural programme, a lot of sports areas. That was an interesting design too.

When I was in charge of the school refurbishments in Nova Iguaçu, we carried out a project which received an award at the *São Paulo Architecture Biennial*.

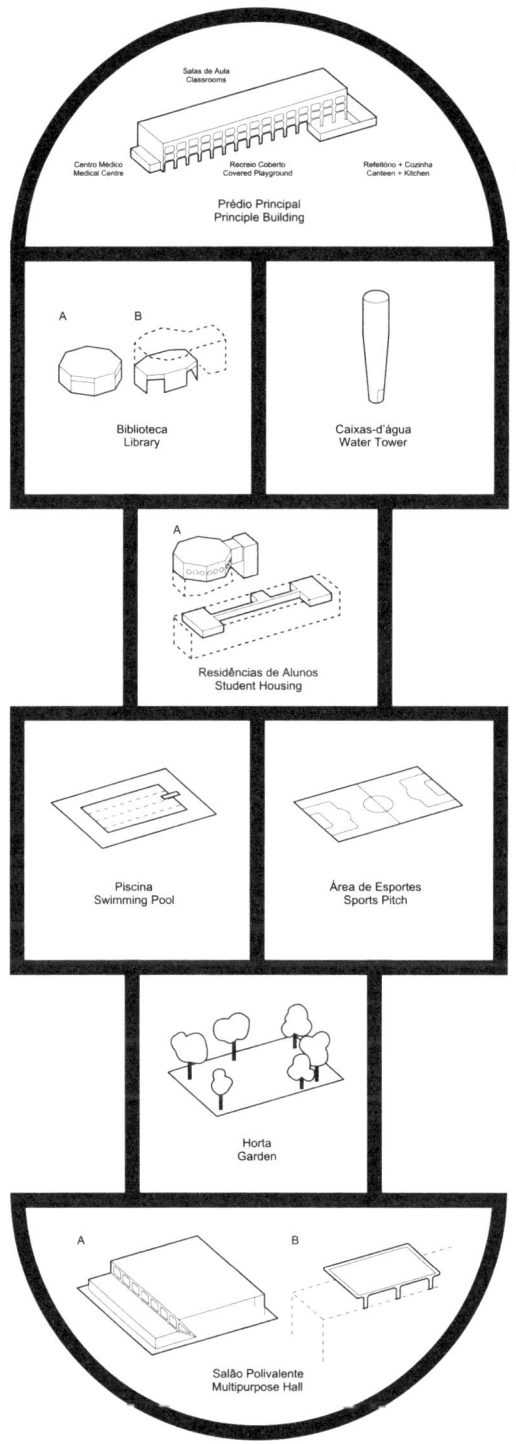

A diagram in the form of a game of amarelinha (Brazilian hopscotch) illustrating the range of different elements composing the CIEP complex

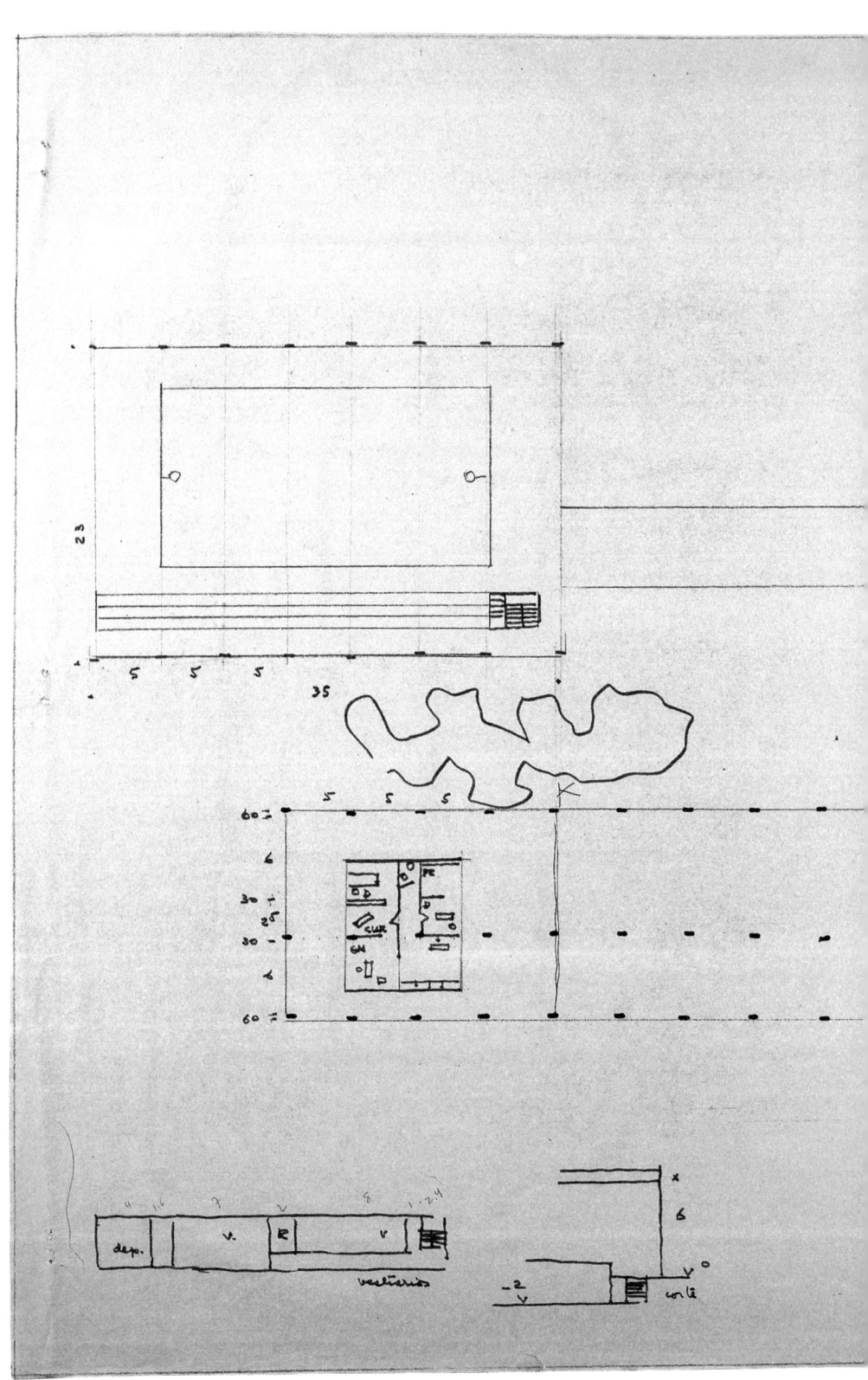

Site plan by Oscar Niemeyer, showing main and auxiliary buildings

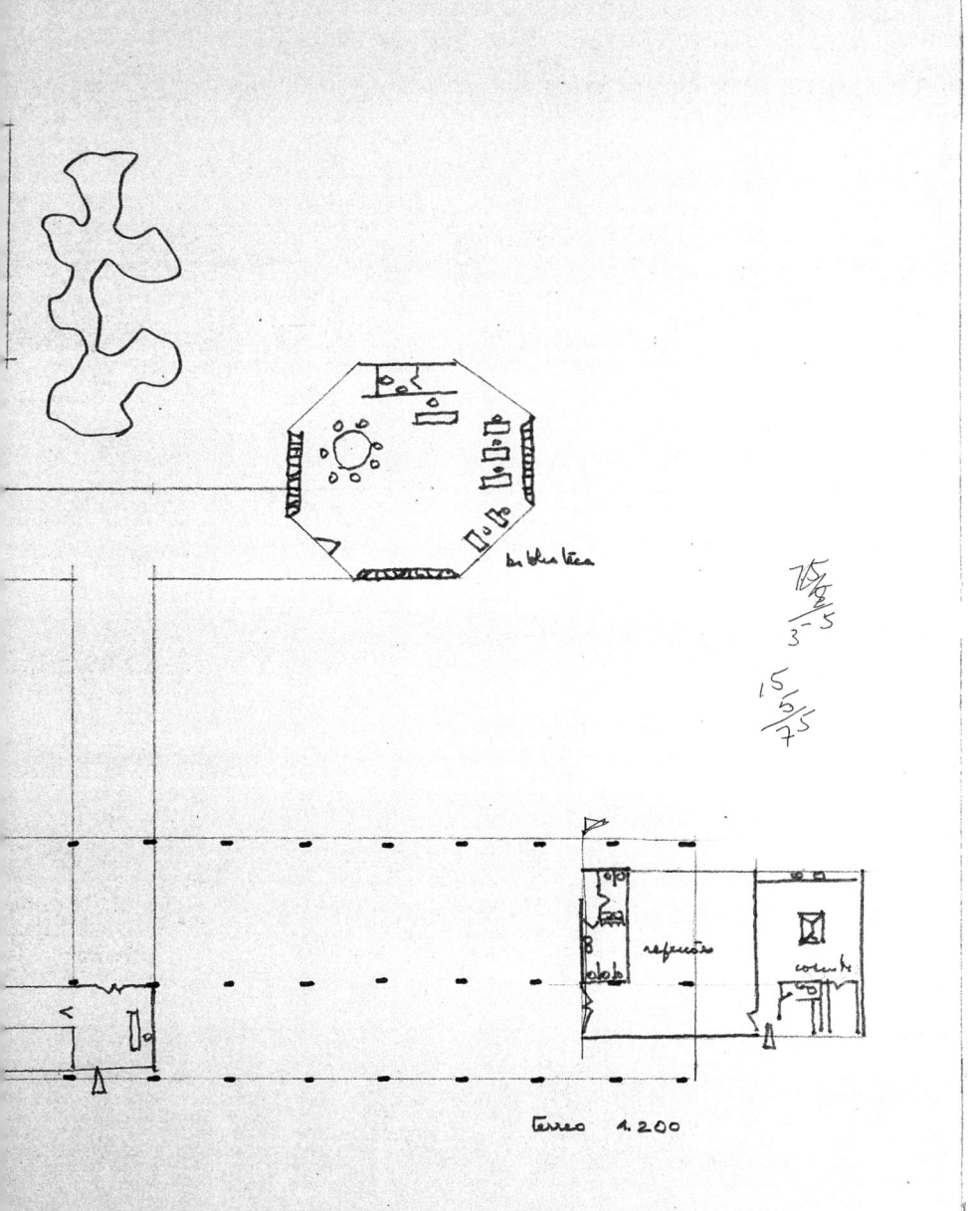

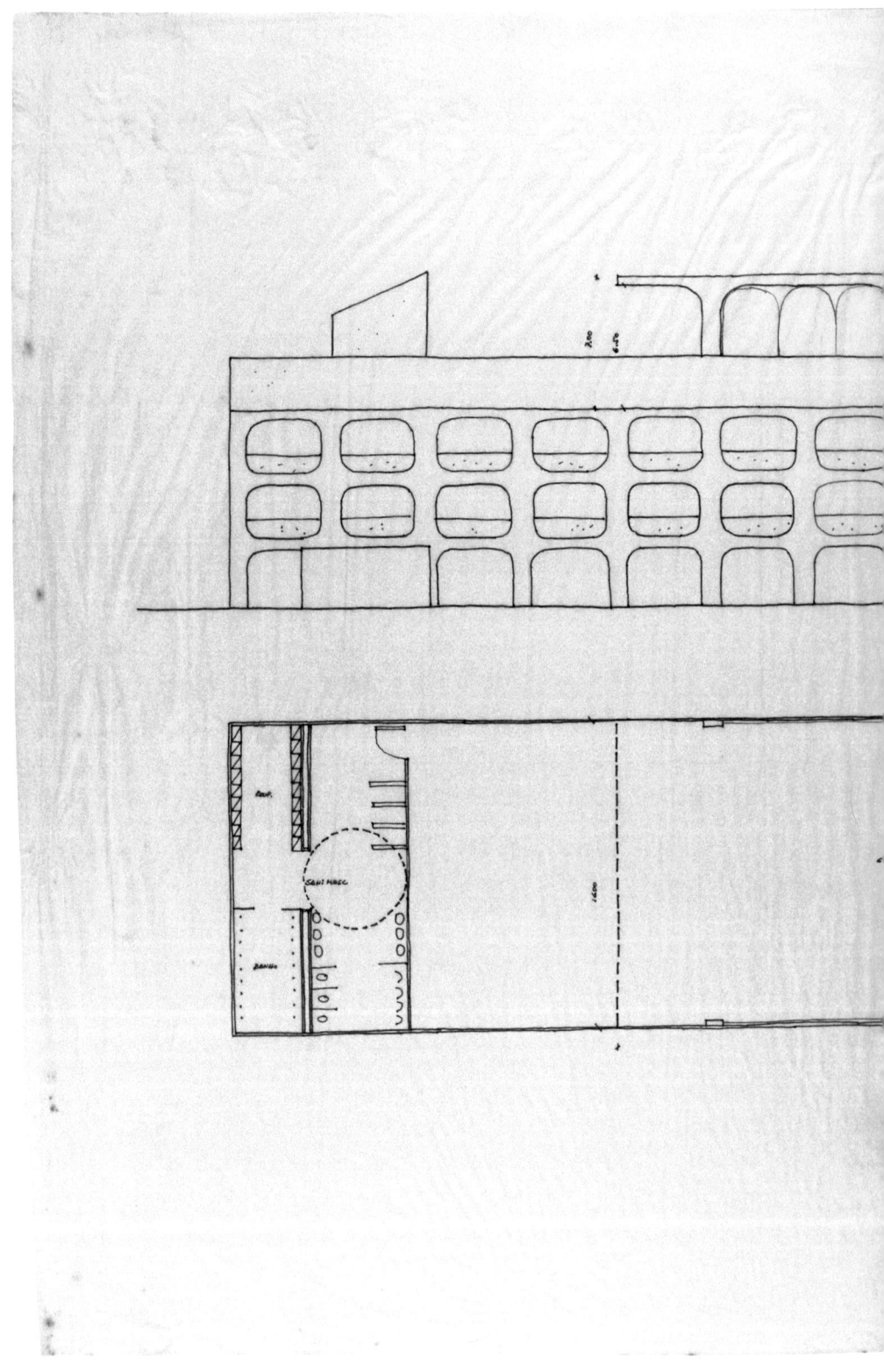

Elevation and plan drawings for a compact CIEP by Oscar Niemeyer

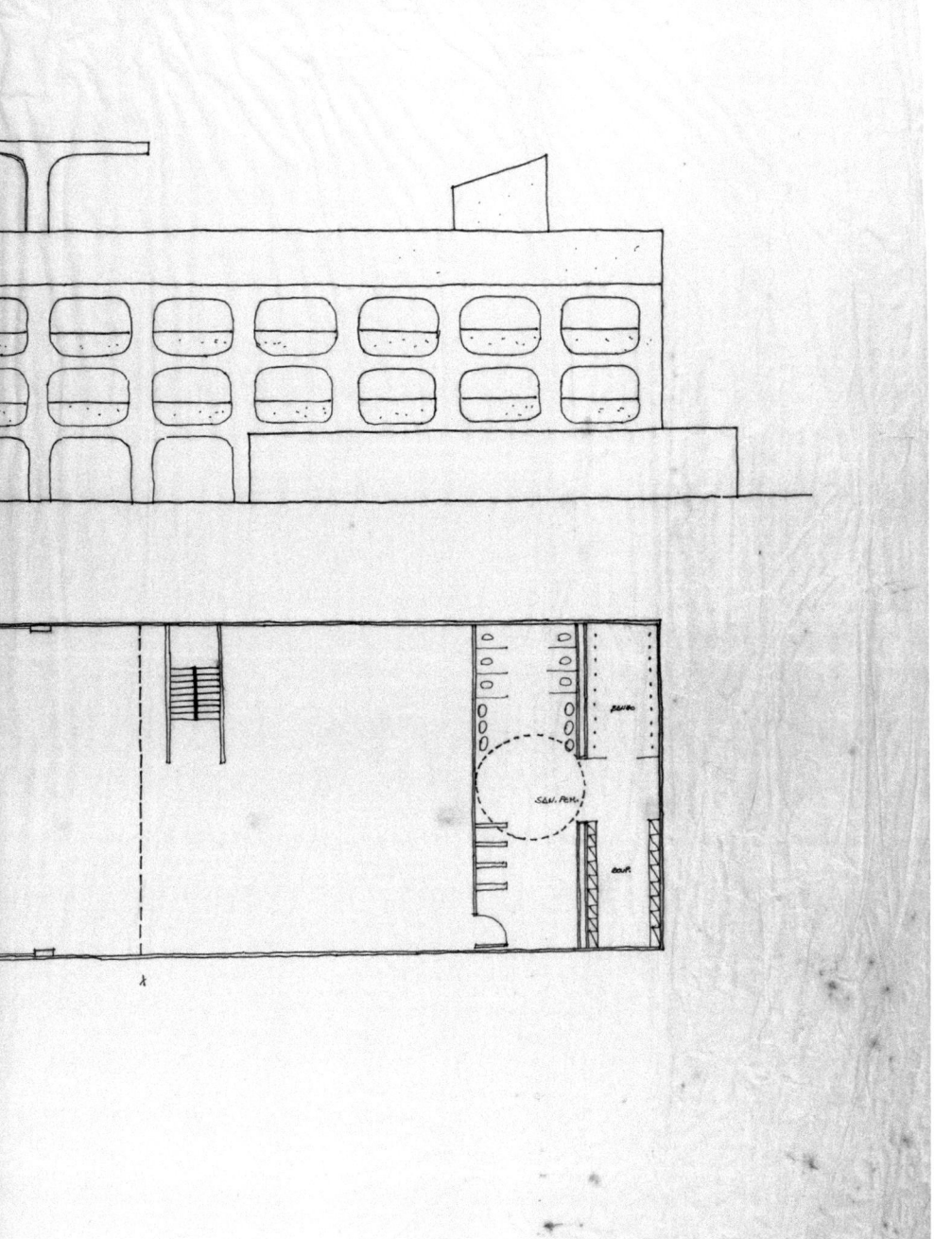

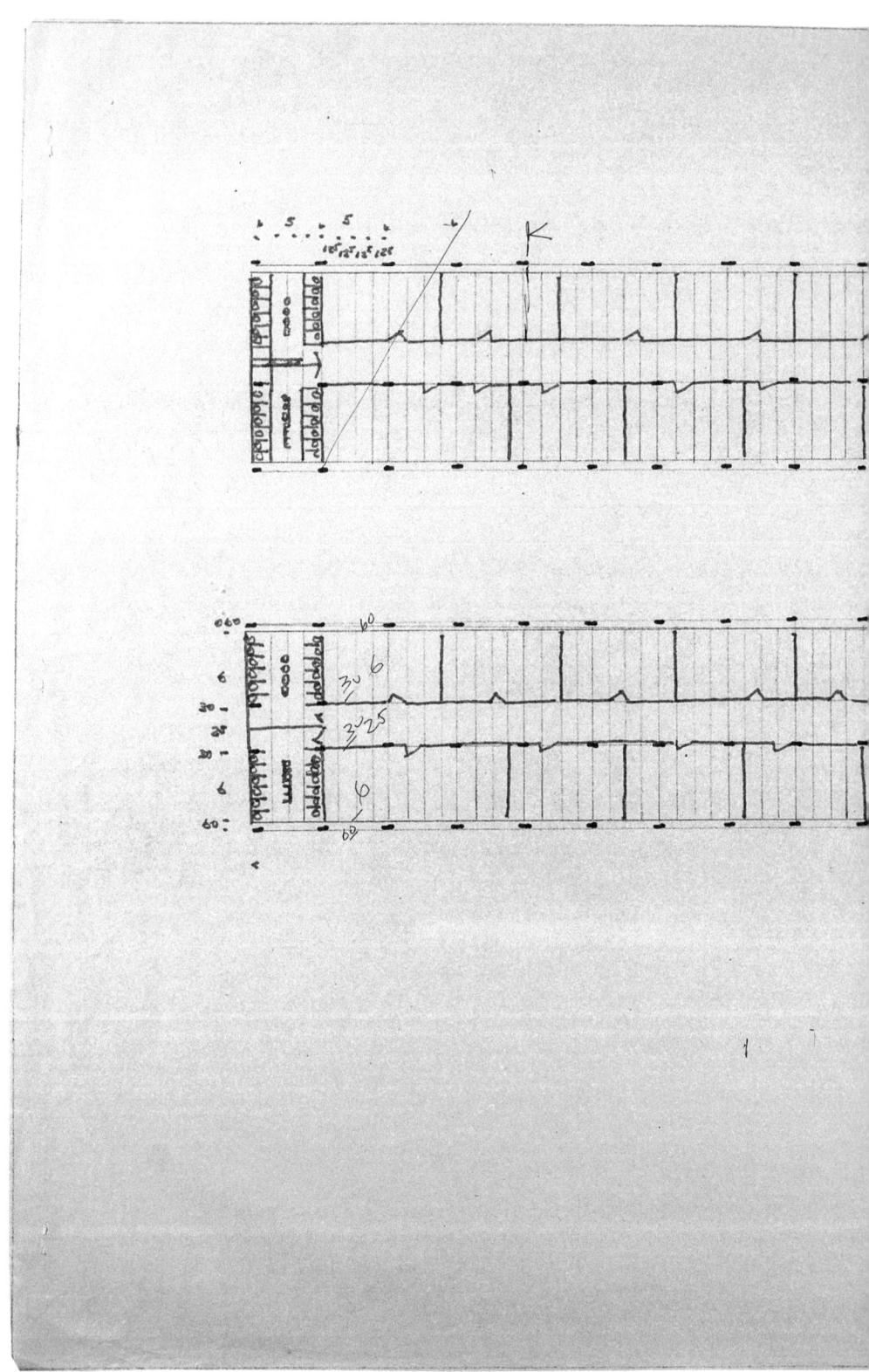

First and second floor plans of the classic CIEP block by Oscar Niemeyer

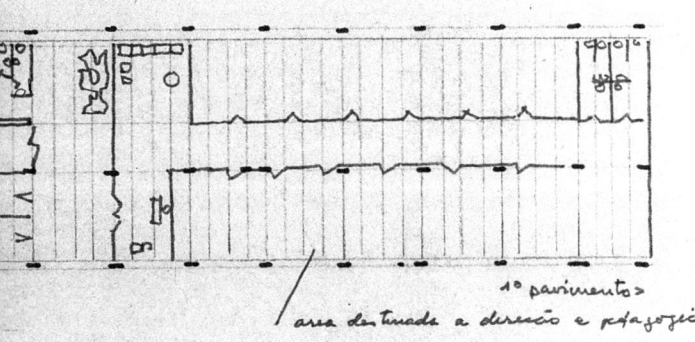

2º pavimento
aulas 87,5 m²

1º pavimento
area destinada a direção e pedagogia a colonizar

A Fabric Of Schools

Nova Iguaçu is a totally peripheral city. But this periphery is an interesting condition, where the school is actually the last survivor in terms of a civic building, of what public space should be. Even in the most terrible place, the poorest town, you will find a school. And it's very strong, sometimes the building is in terrible shape, but there is the idea of a public building. We started mapping these schools and found that sometimes the plot of the school was quite narrow, without any space to do anything new. So then we started mapping empty plots or abandoned squares close to the schools and added the walking distance, like one minute, or five minutes. We started to create solutions—sports areas, or sometimes LAN houses. You know what a LAN house is? A place for internet?

An internet café?

WF   Exactly, exactly. It's very common in favelas to have internet cafes, although now they are starting to disappear as more people have computers in their homes. We created public internet cafés in some of these areas—it was a programme to create a network of activities connected with these schools.

I have a couple of questions for you about the heritage of the CIEPs. As the CIEPs were built from a standardised design, we know that at the beginning of the programme they were basically all the same. But have the architecture and interiors of the CIEPs evolved or adapted over the past 25 years?

WF   You know that all the CIEPS in the city of Rio are listed, they are protected? In fact the entire body of Niemeyer's work is listed. Talking specifically about CIEPs, I think that this is sometimes a problem. To have all of the CIEPs listed makes no sense; it is a standard solution! Sometimes I think it's not a problem to pull down a CIEP to build something else—there are a lot of CIEPs after all. I don't know the internal condition of every single one, but maybe it is a mistaken kind of fetish to protect all of Niemeyer's work. But on the other hand, most of the CIEPs are still in pretty good shape: the façades, the materials—even the windows, far more delicate than the concrete—are usually in good condition. We have a massive number of these buildings; in the suburban areas it might be possible to find abandoned CIEPs, but not in the core of the city. We have CIEPs in Catete and in Lapa, both of which are historic areas, and they work very well within the a density of the population there. The CIEPs are still very helpful to these areas.

Are they allowed to be converted, if they are abandoned? Can they be given a new use?

WF   That is a really interesting idea, but I don't know of any proposals to do that. I think it's a very good idea to consider repurposing this kind of building. There are other kinds of use for CIEPs, I think there is a CIEP attached to a SESC *(Serviço Social do Comércio)*, which is a social and cultural centre run by the Federation of Commerce and Trade. It is the quality of the structure, I think, that makes it possible to imagine other proposals, both internal and architectural developments, but still within the basic structure.

So you mentioned that all the CIEPs have recently been listed. Do you think that this will affect the ability of the schools to be modified?

WF   No, I don't think it will create a problem, because I'm assuming that there is no specific heritage focus to the CIEPs. It's a more detailed approach that makes the selection of some CIEPs. But I don't think that this protection will block new ideas. In fact I would like to see some new ideas! *(laughs)*

If people wanted to make changes to CIEPs, now or in the future, who would sanction that? Would it be the state or would it be Niemeyer's office—do they still have an influence on what people can do?

WF   I don't think there is any permission required from Niemeyer's office. The important thing is to know who owns that CIEP: sometimes it is the state government and sometimes it is the municipality. But I think there are only these two options, there is no non-institutional entity that owns a CIEP.

Maybe special ones could be protected, as case study examples?

WF   Yes, for example the one in Catete was the first school, but it doesn't have the best arrangement. I think there are other CIEPs with more interesting arrangements. Speaking as a heritage consultant, we could have a sort of grading—like a type I CIEP or a type II CIEP—making specific protections of typologies and so on. So you protect examples of these solutions. Because I think it was a wrong approach to list everything by Niemeyer in the same way. When they made this list for protection, I think they forgot about the number of CIEPs!

Yes—he made five hundred school buildings alone! Niemeyer was working on the Sambódromo around the same time, and apparently Darcy Ribeiro had an idea to turn that into a school too, to install classrooms underneath the bleachers—making a stadium school for 15,000 pupils. That sounds really ambitious! Do you know anything about that project? And did it actually happen?

WF   Yes, I think that they took the experience of the CIEPs and used it to do the *Sambódromo*. At that moment it was not possible to fit the whole CIEPs programme within the fabric of that building; they made one very narrow building for the VIP balconies and they used another part of the building as a school. It actually did operate as a school for a long time, but it was not specifically designed to be used as a school in the long term. The school itself stopped operating some years before the construction of the second part of the Sambódromo.

I was interested to hear that one of the Ipanema CIEPs is located in an abandoned hotel. Do you know anything about that?

WF   Oh yes, that one is in fact not a Niemeyer design. The CIEP in Ipanema was a hotel on a hill top. In the 1970s there were a lot of crazy buildings in difficult locations—like that one. There was a lot of public reaction against this kind of building, and so there are many abandoned structures in the hills and in the forest. There was an abandoned building here in Laranjeiras that has been remodelled as a police headquarters now; that building in Ipanema became a school some time after it failed as a hotel. But at least in terms of the architectural solution, it's not a true CIEP!

Ricardo Henriques is a professor of Economics at the Universidade Federal Fluminense, with a specialist focus on inequality, education and social economy. Henriques was formerly president of the prestigious Instituto Pereira Passos (IPP), an advisory institution and grant-providing body focussed on urban planning and municipal policy. He has held advisory and executive positions across several departments within the State of Rio de Janeiro, during which time he developed the UPP Social initiative, following the imposition of the controversial UPP programme in 2010, (Unidade de Polícia Pacificadora, or Police Pacification Unit). The UPP programme aims to control the drug-related violence which affects dozens of unstable, marginalised neighbourhoods and favelas, but the scale of problems makes the UPP Social Initiative intrinsic to any chance of success.

The IPP headquarters, housed within the City Of Rio offices in the leafy neighbourhood of Laranjeiras, produce much of the planning policy, cartographic and statistical research for the City. After the day's work on Monday April 9th, 2012, Henrique elaborated on the CIEPs urban impact, in aesthetic and social senses.

A Conversation with Ricardo Hennriques
    The Economist

RH   At that time in the early 1980s, we had a higher rate of students dropping out than we have today. So the way that the CIEPs try to deal with this, by considering a combined programme of architecture and pedagogy that attracts and keeps children in school—it's a good idea, I think. The standardised building design has some advantages—firstly, it makes for reduced costs, obviously, in terms of construction. But at the same time, it gives a certain global perception, a perception of a standard of quality. Not only of a physical and architectural standard; I mean the perception that the schools themselves may have the same quality. Now, in fact, that is not quite true: in the sense of even though there's a perception of equality there, unfortunately they are not quite equal in the sense of a pedagogical performance.

> But you're saying that the idea of standardisation was seen as a positive thing?

RH   Yes, for sure.

> In the UK, many school buildings built in the 1960s and 1970s were standardised and prefabricated, mostly to save money. Even today standardisation in architecture is often seen as a negative quality.

RH   Yes, that's true, but that's another problem, another discussion. You see, the standardisation of a pedagogical strategy has lots of risks. Actually in Rio and Brazil, when you lose diversity in the curriculum, you lose a lot. So the big challenge is how to customise some elements of learning, while keeping some aspects of a universal strategy—so there is an equivalence, the possibility of promoting some level of equality. From an architectural point of view, one of the most strongest qualities of the CIEPs is that their standardisation produces a perception of equality. In an ideal world, we could have this and at the same time adapt the learning procedures to address children who live in the largest favelas, like Rocinha, compared to children who live in the richer west or the south zones of the city. If you deliver exactly the same standardised pedagogical content, probably you will not find ways to really engage these diverse students. And the challenges in Rio are completely different to the challenges in, for example, Amazônia, so we need to think carefully about where to find an equilibrium. Still now, we are looking for this balance in Brazil; we need some clear standards in mathematics, for example, while at the same time, it would be interesting to have some possibilities of customisation, recognising diverse social questions.

But in looking for this balance between equilibrium and diversity, I personally think that the standardisation in the design of the buildings is helpful. This is in a society that urgently needs to reduce a perception of inequality. I'm not sure what the impact would be—the psychological impact, the subjective impact, the intangible impact—in a society where inequality is not so high, I can't anticipate that. In a society that is as unequal as Brazil, it's really interesting—it's a kind of assurance, to state that from the beginning the opportunities are similar.

> It is really interesting. How far do you think the architecture of the buildings relates to each different site?

RH   In what sense?

> Just to the immediate physical situation. Is there some sense that Niemeyer's design references a sort of vernacular style from within Rio, so that it works in the city context as well as in a rural or suburban context? Or is the design so characteristic that it refuses all context?

RH   Well, that's not so easy to figure out, because by now they have been around for a while. Even if they seemed different once upon a time, over the last few decades they have been completely incorporated into lived space. I think the fact of their sheer quantity, their presence, would produce the same result, even if the design was completely different. I suppose the scale of such a solution would produce the same impact for the city, even if another design was less functional: the impact is one of scale.

> **They are quite large in scale as buildings, and they repeat—they're quite graphic.**

RH   They are interesting, but I'm not an architect—it's difficult for me to say much about their quality in terms of design! They definitely have an impact—the solution of the windows, the fact that space is more horizontally spread out than vertical—it's interesting, but I'm not sure of their value per se.

> **I'm thinking about where they are sited as well—they really stand out in their context, they don't try and hide. For me, I feel that's important, that you really can see where they are.**

RH   That's it. That is important. To have a strong, recognisable design in a sense, no? The CIEPs design has a character, a signature, that is very important. But what I'm saying is, when it's a complete programme with hundreds of buildings, then even if it was a different design it wouldn't matter…

> **… As long as it had a similar characteristic.**

RH   Yes, that's it. The problem of the identity is really important, you can produce an architectural identity that everybody recognises. But I think the recognition is the result of reproduction at scale, rather than the unique design.

> **That is interesting, and understandable—there are, after all, five hundred of them! Is there a larger history of standardisation or prefabrication in Brazilian architecture, or was this one of the first of such projects?**

RH   As far as I know, Governor Leonel Brizola had done something similar in the 1960s, in Rio Grande do Sul, with a completely different kind of design—but it was another standardised school.

> **I heard about that, the other school—something like 6,000 units! How important are the specific surroundings or the landscape in the design of the CIEPs? Do you think the design helps to knit or embed the schools into the community, or does it stay separated?**

RH   There are so many different CIEPs, and as many situations of integration. Have you been to the school in Borel, right? It is completely different: on the side of a hill, and it's not actually inside the favela, it is next door. While the one in Rocinha is completely inside the favela, it's built like that. But I think it is an easy building to be integrated into most sites. If you go to the west zone, where it's completely flat, without hills, you can see one CIEP here, and one there..

> **It's as if in the scale of application of these buildings, they almost becomes a fabric. And it is this fabric of schools which allows the context to come into it.**

RH   Yes, I think it allows it.

An example of a compact CIEP on a difficult site: the CIEP Doutor Bento Rubião in Rocinha, Brazil's largest favela

Carlos Niemeyer de Medeiros is the Director of the Fundação Oscar Niemeyer (Oscar Niemeyer Foundation), based in Rio de Janeiro. As his name suggests, he is also the famous architect's great-grandson and bears part of the responsibility for the maintenance of his built and unbuilt legacy. The Foundation provides support and technical advice to the execution of works, the preservation and restoration of spaces designed by Oscar Niemeyer. As director, Carlos also acts as the curator and custodian of a significant part of Oscar Niemeyer's archive of drawings, photographs, publications and personal attributes. Carlos Niemeyer is also an architect and a tenured professor of Civil Construction at the Instituto Federal São Paulo.

The Fundaçao Oscar Niemeyer, established in 1988, is hidden behind an innocuous looking door on a quiet street in Glória. We met Carlos on Tuesday April 10th, 2012, to peruse the collection of photographs and original drawings, particularly the concept-books and storyboards so characteristic of Oscar Niemeyer, and to look for clues connecting the CIEPs to other design projects or concepts in the archive.

A Conversation with Carlos Niemeyer
> The Archivist

Out of interest, how much material do you keep?

CN Oh, more than 4,000 drawings and original sketches, and probably 10,000 technical drawings…

Do you think the CIEPs was seen as a sort of strange side-project? Why isn't there much archival material about the programme?

CN Because Niemeyer was not used to documenting everything like that. The way he would work is like this: he used to draw the concept of the buildings and the forms, he would draw ideas and then he would give them to his team to develop. Actually he would draw and also write about the project; it was kind of an album that he used to produce, with both drawings and writings, to show his clients. Most of the material we have is from these albums, and mainly from projects that were never built. Probably for the CIEPs he designed a concept for the project. The CIEPs was planned to be very widely applied, so probably he would have made one drawing or two, and presented these to Darcy Ribeiro, Leonel Brizola and the other people responsible for the project. Then he would have passed these to the team of engineers and architects who implemented the project—so he would not have kept all the technical drawings. Basically, in the case of CIEPs, there was such a large number of buildings, the technical drawings were made by the companies responsible for the actual construction, so we don't have them.
But the CIEPs programme was a really important work in Niemeyer's portfolio. Partly for its subject—the idea to really change the lives of people in Rio de Janeiro. Unfortunately the government that came after Brizola decided to interrupt the project.

So from Niemeyer's team, who would have worked on it the most?

CN Umm… the architect Jair Valera and José Carlos Süssekind, the engineer, I would guess—both of them were long-time collaborators…

Ah yes. Jair Valera actually told me that there was an idea that if Brizola became president, they were planning to build ten thousand CIEPs all around Brazil.

CN I don't know—they were political, and politics is very complex. But even if Brizola had a political goal, it was a very important project for the population. We would now have a very different situation in terms of education in Rio, because people could work full time, while their children could be studying all day in the school.

Secretary of Education Claudia Costin said they're going to bring back the full-time education programme.

CN They should do that, it is necessary. Darcy Ribeiro was a very intelligent man and we would have another situation in Rio de Janeiro if the programme wasn't stopped for political reasons.

I also asked Jair what projects, if any, had influenced the CIEPs' design—either within Niemeyer's own working history, or any other projects from outside. He said that with Niemeyer, every project is a new project. From curating the archive, can you see any influence on the CIEPs?

CN No, I don't remember anything like that… It is as Jair said, he always tried to make things different. He tried to implement something in specific projects, an idea that maybe didn't go ahead and sometimes, you see that coming in another one. In the case of CIEPs, I don't remember if there was anything like that? This coffee has a bit of canela, how do you say that?

Cinnamon?

CN   (Drinks coffee) This was a material he produced to make an exhibition. There is a note written here, 'The programmes are different but when they have economy and urgency as their goal, they should be modular, repetitive and prefabricated'. He writes here that study environments should be simple, something repeatable.

    But this isn't the CIEP project, is it?

CN   The concept of the CIEPs is somehow in there… Here is a poem about his work. It says, it's not the straight angle that attracts me…

    … I always found this an interesting comment from Niemeyer, which I read in his biography: 'Architecture is an invention, and therefore for a long time I have been forced to justify the different forms I have created.' Does that mean he would design intuitively, and then feel like he had to explain to the clients, 'Yes, it's like this because of so and so…' after designing it?

CN   Because it was always something further than what people expected. I will show you the album of Brasília airport, which was never built; he made a round plan and the military said no, it's not possible to do this. But now, many airports are round.

    What is the meaning of this sketch, the flower and the hand?

CN   This was made as a limited edition print. He was trying to show the important stuff, generosity… He made an association between the flowers of nature and the open hand.

    And what is that project, that looks similar to the CIEPs…

CN   Yes, I wanted to show you this. That's the FATA Engineering Headquarters…
(Fabbrica Automazione Trasporti e Affini, Turin, 1975)

    Oh yes, in Italy—Turin, right?

CN   Yes, the FATA in Torino, it was made a few years after the building for Mondadori. That one has a different distance between the columns and here they have the same.

    Were there any models, or maquettes? I've got a book with a photograph of a model, but maybe it's in Darcy Ribeiro's archive…

CN   No, we don't have any models. Niemeyer would usually draw, and the necessity of explanation became really a process of working. He used to draw then write, and then he sometimes would realise that he had to change the project.

    So he would make a storyboard, like a brochure of the project for the client, with these sort of steps?

CN   Yes, like one, two, three…

    But he didn't make a storyboard or an album for the CIEPs?

CN   Probably he made them for the CIEPs too, but we don't have them. Most of what we have are materials from his unbuilt projects, because usually the clients wanted to keep the albums. This book was published by the Rio de Janeiro government about the *Sambódromo*… Probably this was the album that Niemeyer made.

    Jair told me that the Sambódromo was made in three months, from design to construction—just three months!

CN   Yes, three months from start to finish, ending on the day of the carnival!

    That's amazing! So, were these spaces under the bleachers intended as classrooms? Did it actually operate as a school?

CN   I'm not sure. But I think so.

    Ha, no one is sure! And this was also prefabricated, right—because they were built at the similar time, the CIEPs, weren't they? *(Looking at drawings)* **It seems that the Sambódromo was almost part of the CIEPs project, there seems to be a relationship.**

CN   The politicians made a very bad mistake by interrupting the CIEPs project.

The main block of each CIEP contains about twenty classrooms of various sizes, originally fitted out with specially designed bright yellow furniture

One thing that keeps coming up is whether it was a good thing that the CIEPs was seen as a very political statement. Because Leonel Brizola, Oscar Niemeyer, and Darcy Ribeiro were all very socialist and their ideas were very bold, very prominent.

I was thinking that maybe because the programme was so bold, it actually made it quite easy for the next government to react against it, because the CIEPs were so strongly associated with Brizola. Even though the CIEPs were part of an amazing project, politically the next party kind of had to get rid of them. In hindsight, do you think it was a good idea to make such a bold statement?

CN   I think you should, but you need to take care about this. The problem is when you do something on this scale, it's impossible to separate the idea from the person who begins the project. I think projects like this should not be personal or tied to someone, because then there is this risk.

I don't know if you know the project in Barra de Tijuca, the *Cidade de Música*? This was a project that was pushed forward by the mayor there, but then when the next administration came, they tried to change the building to an art centre instead—just to avoid the association with the previous guy. I don't know what I would do if I was a governor or whatever after Brizola. But the problem is that maybe Brizola was wrong in the way he used this programme politically. It worked against him, and later against the programme itself—maybe that's a good lesson.

It's such a shame, of course. Obviously there was so much time and money invested in the CIEPs programme, for it to be neglected so soon.

CN   The most incredible thing is that this programme was made to benefit the population, the people really needed this. And when the new government came in place of Brizola, the media was so strongly set against Brizola that it succeeded in making the people change their minds. These were people who should have wanted Brizola again, because the most important issue after health is education, but they decided to put another guy there instead.

Jair was suggesting they—Brizola and Ribeiro—knew that they had to build the CIEPs fast, because they only had four years in government. They suspected that Brizola might not get re-elected, but I think they thought that the project itself would survive, because surely once the people had seen them, they would demand more, they would not want to let them go. Obviously they were surprised.

CN   It's something that is difficult to forget: there's a building, a project, an educational programme, something that nobody can argue against… It's incredible, what happened. It's a crime, it's unbelievable, it's not possible. But then… Each people gets the government it deserves! *(laughter)*

Although I get the sense that maybe, enough time has passed. I was speaking to Claudia Costin, she told me the City is planning to bring back the full-time education programme and a lot of the ideas that Brizola had originally pursued. Perhaps the CIEPs are becoming less associated with Brizola?

CN   Since he died, also.

Yes, since he died, the political climate is changing and now maybe the CIEPs can be reclaimed by other governments.

CN   Yeah. It's a difficult thing, you need to find the way to make the people implement the educational programme. But it would not be done specifically through the CIEPs.

Ah, because the new government would not want to show the old programme as being too successful, right? Obviously she said they've been starting to look after the buildings, painting them for example. They are such robust buildings that even if you just paint them, they immediately look great again.

CN   The form is like… Well, the form is there, you can't change it. The political issues are tougher to resolve. But I think the United Kingdom would not have this problem.

There's an interesting difference. Historically in the UK, the idea of repetition or standardisation is generally seen as negative. But in this project, it definitely seems like repetition was seen as something positive. There was an idea that every community starts from the same place and has the same standard of building and the same standard of education: at least, the idea is very democratic.

CN   Maybe you could have the basic building and also have elements that would change—not in the moment of implementation but maybe something that you can adapt over time…

I was thinking about that, in some of the additional buildings…

CN   Maybe one or two could be different… I don't know, I'm not an architect!

Lauro Cavalcanti is an architect, anthropologist and writer who has spent the last two decades researching modern architecture in Brazil. He is the Director of Paço Imperial, an historic cultural centre in Rio de Janeiro. He was the curator of the exhibition ConVivência, for the Brazil Pavilion at the Venice Biennale of Architecture in 2012, which featured an installation inspired by the work of the pioneering modernist Lucio Costa alongside the office of contemporary practitioner Marcio Kogan. He has written several books on architecture, aesthetics and society including Moderno e Brasileiro (2006).

We visited Lauro on Monday April 9th, 2012, the day after Easter Sunday. After a tour of both the Paço Imperial's temporary art exhibitions and historical spaces, and before continuing our discussion over lunch in the restaurant, we talked in Lauro's office. Lauro's perspective is refreshingly critical—not only taking into account the social and political rhetoric behind the CIEPs intentions, but appraising the performance and reception of the CIEP buildings within the city's architectural fabric.

A Conversation with Lauro Cavalcanti
   The Curator

LC   At the time that the CIEPs were built here, they were also highly criticised because there was already a whole network of old schools which were not used all the time. Many people felt that the government was messing up by confusing the priority of education with the impetus to make new buildings. With the CIEPs project, it was felt necessary to dignify the lives of the children and so on. Also to reinforce the teachers who were already engaged, some believed that all the major changes to their way of doing things, would have a positive effect. Have you visited any of the CIEPs?

Yes. We've been to the CIEPs in Catete, in Borel… Rocinha, the one at the bottom and the one at the top, and another in Lapa.

LC   And how are they working?

Inside they seem good, everyone seems pleased. I think there are issues with the half-height walls, because of the noise. I spoke to Claudia Costin, the education secretary, and she was saying that she had only heard of one school where the half-walls worked, and that was because the teachers had received special training.

LC   It's like the architecture school that Mies made in the United States…

So they are being modified now—apparently there's an official way of building the half-walls up, which involves installing louvres to maintain ventilation. Some of the schools have said it's too expensive, so they've found their own temporary solutions…

I wanted to ask you something: I met with Washington Fajardo, who tried to describe how the architecture of the schools referenced an urban vernacular of Rio de Janeiro, and that this allowed them to integrate in whatever context they were in…

LC   Hmm… I don't understand what CIEPs have to do with the vernacular.

Well, that's the question – do you think the design has anything to do with a sense of a particular Rio vernacular?

LC   No, I don't think so. I think it was meant to be an example, a practical process to set a civilising example, instead of an anthropological or ethnological approach. In Brazil, we always deal with those two tendencies, one is more practical, civic, in a way to set examples and to develop things from there, while the other is more ethnological, seeing the way people build. The main person driving the project was Darcy Ribeiro, the vice governor and also an anthropologist…

Yes, we are already talking to the Darcy Ribeiro Foundation.

LC   So you know his ideas. But it was always like that, a matter of civilisation and setting standards. Niemeyer, for instance: people always asked him in a sort of nagging way, if that's the right word—why, despite being a Communist, had he not made any social housing or schools? His answer was that he did not believe architecture would change society, and that this work was the work of a revolution, the citizen and of engagement via movements and so on. And that he would not wish to impoverish his architecture and knowledge through an act of demagogy.
It is a very interesting because the two architects who did not believe in this transformative role of architecture were both Communists: Niemeyer, a Stalinist, and Vilanova Artigas who was also Communist but from another wing, not Trotskyist—you'd have to check that, I'm not positive. Niemeyer said he would only do such a project if there was a government in which he believed, and that was the case at that moment.

In fact it was a very specific moment, also because you had an amnesty, the return of politicians and intellectuals who had been exiled abroad, the first free election for governors… So there was all these symbolic actions going on.

> **It seems to me that the project is quite radical in a way, lots of new ideas—it is quite experimental. There has to be a certain type of government to enable that, a strong government. Would you say that at that time the Brizola government was particularly strong?**

LC   The local government was leftist. Brizola had two terms but in his first term he was quite determined to set things up… But many CIEPs were discontinued, if you drive out past Niterói, towards Búzios, you see many abandoned ones. I fully understand that sometimes, to do something really big, a big programme, you cannot rely on the existing structures, I do believe that. But on the other hand, not trying actually to improve or work with the existing… Both things should have been done, in parallel…
I say that I understand, because I worked on another cultural programme that belongs to the civil service; I must confess I am not familiar with the consequences from the CIEPs exactly. Around that time I was working as an anthropologist—I had a Bachelor's degree in architecture but then I did my PhD in social anthropology, so technically I have spent more time training in anthropology. There was a literacy foundation called MOBRAL which taught people to read, write and so on, but we were confronted with the fact that children who had attended pre-school classes with MOBRAL were somehow achieving worse grades then ordinary children. The aim of our research was to find out why that was the case, and so I had much contact with people on the education programme.
One thing that I have mixed feelings about… I like very much the work of Niemeyer—and you must have met people who don't, but I do for the most part—most of it was of very good quality architecture, for Brazil it was a miracle. But on the other hand, I don't like politicians using architecture as a logo or mixing things up, so that priority for education shifts to building schools. And that's the rule in Brazil, not only in Rio. Because to be candid, the schools appear, people can see them…

> **They're even quite graphic, in the way that they're inserted…**

LC   Yeah. I always wonder, if they invested that money on teacher training and other things—maybe a balance, at least. I understand also that the schools before were old, there was also a matter of making the poorer areas feel more dignified. But then you have created two divisions again, the areas that receive the CIEPs, and those that don't. So there is a new social class, even within the poorer areas: the people who could go to CIEPs and the people who went somewhere else. And then you create the *pistolão*, you know, when you go through your personal connections to do something…

> **That's a really interesting angle. There seems to be a really strong connection between the new curriculum, the new programme and the architecture. But to pick up on your idea of using the existing, there's a project where a hotel in Ipanema has been changed into a CIEPs. How do you feel about the idea of reusing spaces like that?**

LC   Oh yes, that was very nice, doing that. Look, on the whole, the CIEPs programme, I would say it was positive, but we are only seeing a few details. In the long run, it is a pity the government didn't invest its money in people as much as it does on architecture. It's not only a problem of the CIEPs programme; there were several things like this. There was a federal version of the CIEPs (the CIACs) and I don't know if that worked out well either. The worst thing in Brazil is that successive governments do not tend to continue what the other has started. You don't have the same sense of responsibility and continuity in public policy.

Because the CIEPs programme seemed very much discontinued and run down?

LC   Yes, yes. You see, the CIEPs, in the common perception, were strongly connected to Brizola and his party. So after Brizola, the programme was almost discontinued. Now, for example, there's the City of Music in Barra, the *Cidade das Música (opened as the Cidade das Artes in 2014)*, a signature building by Christian de Portzamparc, which has several problems. The Mayor has decided to transform it into a City of Culture now, for reasons of small politics.

The CIEPs project picks up on a couple of really widespread issues, most of all producing a really rapid and standardised building solution. I read the CIEPs were in a way a response to the mass migration to the cities…

LC   I don't really think so, because of when it was. Urban migration was a fact for Rio until the 1970s, but not so much in the 1980s; at that time all the immigration went to São Paulo, which was the wealthiest city. I think it was just the determination of the City Government here, they decided to do it…

Brizola had also made another version of the schools programme, didn't he? When he was the mayor of another city? Apparently he did a school project there, much larger in scope but with less ambitious architectural design.

LC   He was the governor of Rio Grande do Sul, and the brother-in-law of the President when the military dictatorship started; he tried to mount an armed resistance there, at the time of the coup. When he came back from exile, he decided to live in Rio because it was much more important. You see, he believed that he would be able to become the president… But in the end, he came in third place (to Fernando Collor de Mello in 1990). And so the CIEPs was a sort of demonstration of what could be done in the country, on a national scale… Pretty much, more than a response to the actual conditions. Now, what do you think about getting something to eat?

Yes, sure.

Chapter 4
The Equation To Be Solved

Production capacity at this CIEP factory reached 1.5 schools per week; concrete mixers churned up to 300 cubic metres of concrete each day

Rio de Janeiro's Special Programme of Education demanded schools that would be easy to construct and economical to replicate, state-wide. Brizola and Ribeiro had planned ambitious changes, but held only one term in political office to deliver their vision, with Niemeyer's help. The answer was found in reinforced concrete technology, as seen in the monumental modern cityscapes of the Soviet Union. Concrete was chosen for its strength and resistance; as the prevalent building material in Brazil at the time, it was also possible to harness the primary expertise of local construction companies.

In Brazil, the architect João Filgueiras Lima, known popularly as Lelé, was one of the first to experiment with precast concrete and design schools in rural Brazil. Having visited one of these examples, Brizola and Ribeiro invited Lelé to open the Fábrica de Escolas, a factory of schools in the centre of Rio. This factory produced reinforced concrete elements used to build the Casas da Criança (Children's Houses) and the Escolas Isoladas (Isolated Schools), both of which were parts of the Special Programme.

The CIEPs, however, were not built at the Fábrica. With the assistance of engineer José Carlos Süssekind, Niemeyer developed a new prefabrication system which won the support of all the major private contractors in the state of Rio. Each contractor received an allocation of schools to build, and under the coordination of architect Dr João Otavio Goulart Brizola, effectively built their own regional branches of the Fábrica for the production of concrete elements. Each contractor therefore had direct access to the complete array of concrete elements required. These factory-made components were then transported to various sites across the state and rapidly fitted together. The technology used to manufacture the components required minimal technical knowledge, which enabled factories to employ an 80% unskilled workforce. In this way, the construction programme addressed employment issues within deprived communities, as well as keeping costs down. Additionally, these regional factories produced a broader civic infrastructure for poorer communities, including bus stops and benches.

Under construction: the four main structural elements of a typical CIEP were cast in concrete at factories distributed across the state

José Carlos Süssekind is a structural engineer, teacher and author of several textbooks on structural analysis. A frequent collaborator, Süssekind acted as technical manager for the engineering works required by many of Oscar Niemeyer's ambitious and large-scale designs. The engineer's role is often underplayed or unsung, in favour of the architect —however Süssekind's role is particularly worth noting, as Niemeyer's signature style and visionary designs often required the invention of new building techniques, not to mention a fair degree of engineering experimentation, innovation and invention.

A long-term partnership and friendship formed between the engineer and the architect, forged while Süssekind was still a trainee; over four decades, their collaborations included the construction of works including the Sambódromo Marquês de Sapucaí, the CIEPs schools, the National Museum of Brasília and the University of Constantine, in Algeria. Interestingly, these four projects shared certain principles regarding the use of prefabricated concrete, and provided large scale urban interventions which act as civic fabric as well as architectural objects.

Our Team
>José Carlos Süssekind, The Engineer

When the construction of the *Passarela do Samba* was completed, along with the taste of victory and accomplishment of a whole team that had bonded closely, we retained a desire not to break those bonds—both human and professional—in the certainty that we had formed a group capable of carrying forward yet more daring achievements.

With great joy, then, did we see Governor Leonel Brizola hire the same group shortly afterwards—Oscar Niemeyer, João Otávio Brizola, always under the command of Darcy Ribeiro—to design and oversee the execution of CIEPs, the goal of which is to build, by March 1987, 500 units throughout the state, with a building area exceeding an incredible value of 350,000 square metres!

Reconciling low cost, beauty, functionality and speed of execution: this was the equation to be solved (in our view, definitively through the architectural design). The CIEPs are built entirely from prefabricated products made in concrete, including pillars, slabs and facades—an essential factor towards the achievement of the programme's basic goals. Today, with sixty buildings already delivered, a hundred more nearing completion and another 140 at the beginning of construction, we can categorically state that we have indeed found a solution of maximum architectural dignity, which costs about 30% less than a conventional building of the same size. This is a truly significant number, which attests unequivocally to the care and critical spirit that guided the design and detailing of the project as well as the intense supervision and management controls, well conducted by the Projectum and FAPERJ teams. *(Fundação Carlos Chagas Filho de Amparo à Pesquisa do Estado do Rio de Janeiro)*

As always, there must be space to compliment the important engagement of the construction companies. Enthusiastically they launched into the production of prefabrication plants, casting ten metre columns and slabs of up to 20 square metres for the main building of each CIEP, in addition to the elegant 23 metre beams that span the gymnasium. With each completed building, our admiration grows for their creativity, which translates into progressive gains in the schedule, as do the improvements they have introduced to our systems of transport and installation.

We take part in a great enterprise: great in terms of the huge number of built works; great also because we have realised the meaning of being able—making appropriate use of the design and management concepts that we have—to contribute, by doing what we love, towards the production of viable buildings, capable of transforming education, health and culture. To ensure access to dignified living conditions and the right to dream about a possible future, for a huge number of children, in one of the most important states of the Federative Republic of Brazil.

Originally published in 'O Livro Dos Cieps', (Bloch Editores S.A, 1986), a book intended to act as a manual for the CIEPs initiative.

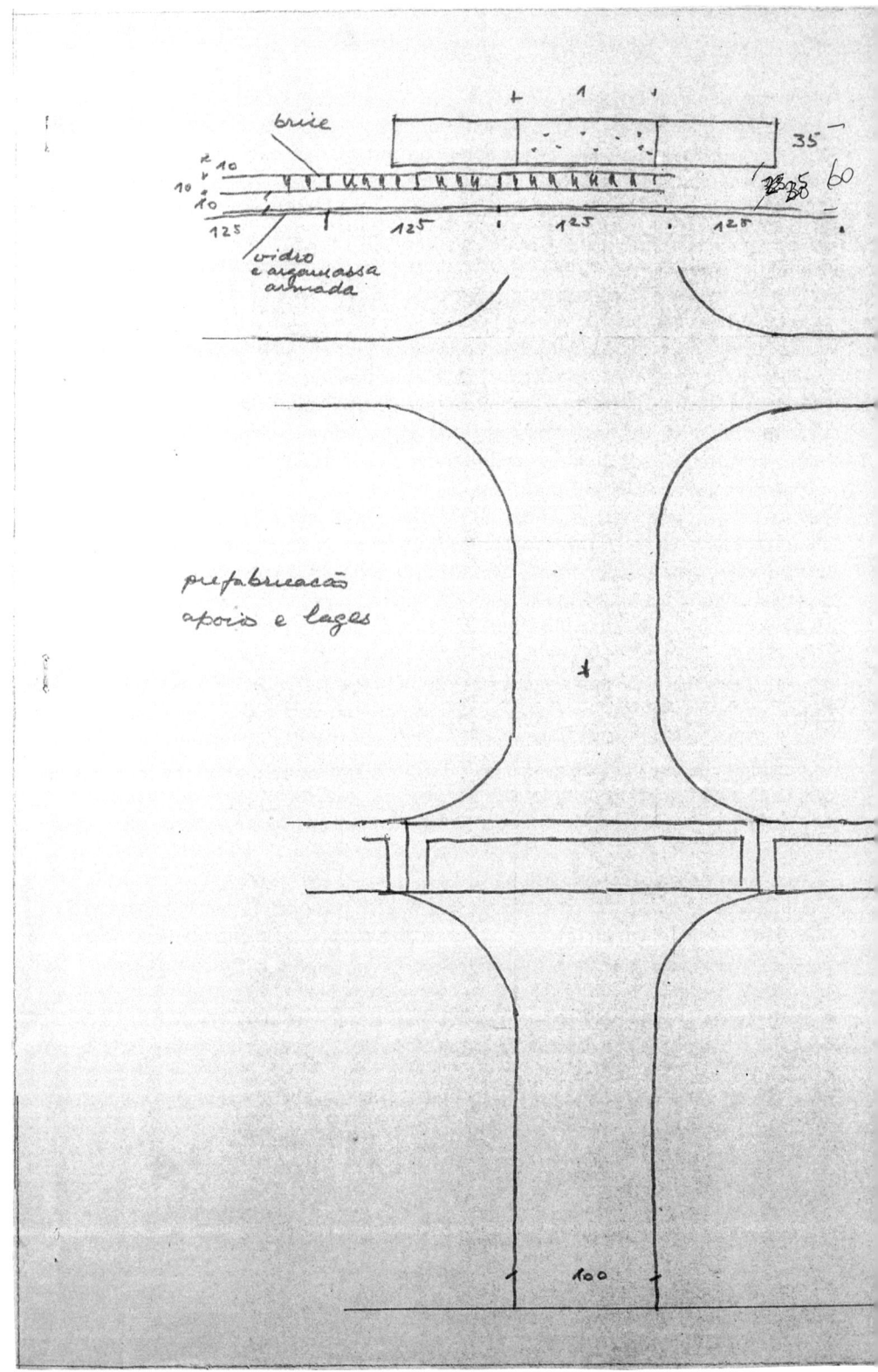

Concrete pillars and slab components for the CIEPs by Oscar Niemeyer

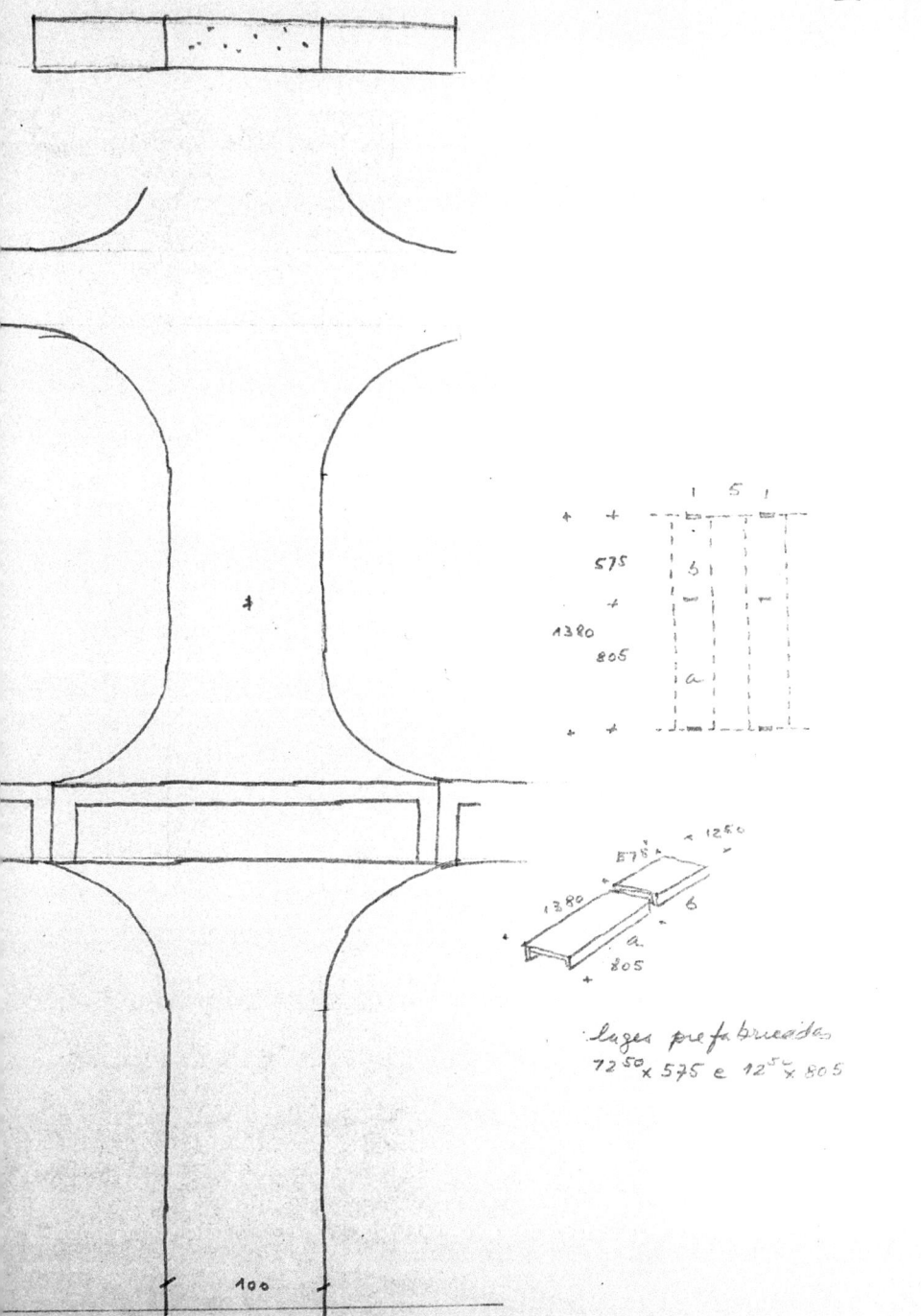

lages prefabricadas
72.50 × 575 e 12.50 × 805

 Jair Rojas Valera is a practicing architect and was a long-time collaborator of legendary Brazilian architect Oscar Niemeyer. Having worked with the master for over thirty years, until the time of his death, Valera continues to lead Niemeyer's architectural practice, together with the latter's granddaughter Ana Elisa Niemeyer. Currently, Valera and Niemeyer Jr. are completing three of Oscar Niemeyer's projects in the states of Rondônia, Minas Gerais and Rio de Janeiro, using sketches and other posthumous materials.

We met in Jair's office in Centro, the downtown part of Rio de Janeiro on Tuesday April 10th, 2012, a few hot days after Easter. Benefitting from his unique and intimate proximity to the master architect, we discussed Niemeyer's working methods and approaches; his attitude towards social methods, the ways he used to engage with clients, and the comparable relationship and independent directions of individual design projects within the office. This discussion on Niemeyer's oeuvre took place overlooking Flamengo Park, designed in 1962 by Niemeyer's modernist contemporaries, the architect Affonso Eduardo Reidy and landscape designer Roberto Burle Marx.

A Conversation with Jair Valera
The Architect

JV   You know that Brazilian schools start early in the morning and finish at midday? But Darcy Ribeiro, who was one of the main instigators of the CIEPs' programme, wanted the children to start school at 8am and leave at 7pm in the evening. So they had breakfast, lunch and dinner, and would go back home already fed. The school provided all their educational needs, but the intention was also that there would be a lot of sports, health, other things. A place for kids to stay for the whole day, learning full time.

> **And what did that mean for the architecture itself?**

JV   From the architectural side, the most important thing was to design a school that was easy to build, and that could be reproduced in great numbers within the shortest time possible. In the State Government of Rio de Janeiro, your term only lasts four years. With this in mind, Niemeyer designed the whole school as a prefabricated structure, made of components. The Government called all the major construction companies in the State and got the support of the whole industry—in fact, not just from the construction companies but also from the developers.

Each contractor got lots, like a certain number of schools to build. Each of them had to set up a central factory to produce the prefabricated elements. So these prefabricated pieces were produced in the central factory and then transported to the construction site to be built. The number of prefabricated pieces was small compared to the school size—the whole system was very well designed, using a limited number of elements. With that system, during the first four years of Brizola's term, 250 schools were built. In the second government term, another 200 schools were built. So I imagine that today there are 450 schools, more or less, around Rio de Janeiro.

> **And why do they look like they do? I'm quite interested in the graphic character of the forms.**

JV   That is really Oscar Niemeyer's distinctive style of architecture, even though it is a pre-fabricated design. It is obviously much more limited in terms of its creative potential, as any pre-fabrication system is. In reality, it is all made in concrete; that way it can be a stronger architecture, more solid, more resistant, and could also fit in to different sites. A real difficulty we had at the time was finding sites to build the schools. So we made three different variations of school design. In the smaller sites, we would place just the main building. In the medium-sized sites, there would be a main building plus a library, and in the biggest ones there could be the main building of the school, a library and a sports court. The architecture basically was determined by everything I just explained. A prefabricated system so it could be as cheap as possible. The architecture was just a conjunction of all these factors. In the end, that's the result.

> **Do you think that Niemeyer was influenced, in his design for the CIEPs, by other projects? Either his own projects or even other people's projects?**

JV   There is no influence between any of Oscar Niemeyer's projects. He is not inspired by any other project. One reason for the uniqueness of his architecture is precisely because it is never based on anything that was already built. For any kind of architecture, he prefers not to know the standards of how things are typically built, or if there is any existing model of it. He creates his own model.

> **In his autobiography, Niemeyer talks about the beauty of nature, and how it multiplies everywhere, whilst maintaining a structural logic. Do you think the CIEPs have been influenced by such thoughts?**

The CIEPs were composed of four main structural elements: the pillars supporting the main building; the pillars for the outdoor multipurpose room; the slabs that sit on the pillars and the Y-shaped beams, nicknamed 'gaivotas' or seagulls, which were specially designed for the outdoor multipurpose rooms.

Production was intense. In one 250 metre long area of the factory, 14 concrete 'seagulls'—enough for one CIEP—could be produced in just ten days. In another section of the factory, 600 men were able to produce 74 slabs and 22 pillars each and every day. Each of the pieces could weigh up to 14 tons and measured up to 11 metre long, in the case of the pillars for the main building. The elements were either stored vertically or placed directly onto a trailer, ready to be transported. All production was controlled by two computers: one used to supervise the progress of the workmen and one to measure the effectiveness of the adapted structures. The incredible rate of construction resulting from the Special Education programme meant that the metropolitan region of Rio de Janeiro had the lowest unemployment levels in the country at that time.

JV   No. I think within the school's façade he included some curved forms, which are a feature of almost all of his works, the curves. He kept this in the façades. But only there: given that all the elements were to be prefabricated, and considering the difficulty and the short time of manufacture, he was obliged to make a somewhat simpler architecture. More streamlined. There are fewer curves.

    In hindsight—if you were going to do it again—what would you change about the project, in terms of the design?

JV   We just made an alteration, because now all the CIEPs are in need of a restoration, as well as an adaptation for the new rules of accessibility and so on. We adapted the original project, and also introduced facilities for computers and other technologies to the building, which did not exist at that time: elevators, air-conditioning. Because the air is very hot, natural ventilation isn't enough: it doesn't help to have a cross-ventilation system if the wind is at 40 degrees! We also had acoustic problems with the original project, but this was all settled in the refurbishments that are being done at the moment. All this is being built right now.

    The fact that the buildings are entirely made of concrete—do you feel that makes it harder to remodel or adapt?

JV   No. Because in Brazil, we don't have the experience that European countries have with steel. There are very few buildings that are built with steel. I think we have a lot more expertise using concrete. The price is also lower, and the durability is higher, right?

    So actually, do you think that originally, the material choice for the CIEPs was taken purely because the workforce had the most experience with concrete?

JV   Yes, that is surely one of the reasons. We had to hire several construction firms, maybe eight or ten companies altogether, and none of them had any previous experience with steel. Concrete is definitely used more often, that is one of the factors. Logically, you would be able to build a steel building in Europe much faster. But here, I am not even sure if there would be enough material for so many schools.

    Was there any difference in the quality of the different construction companies? Did any of the companies build better CIEPs than others?

JV   Yes, there is always some variation. Some of the companies were more adapted to certain prefabricated systems, and others less so. But because the amount was huge, we created a supervisory structure of over 120 people, just to try to maintain the same level of quality and to ensure as much standardisation as possible.

    Was there enough expertise in Rio or did companies have to be brought in from other parts of Brazil?

JV   No, we had enough people to work on this project.

    Were there any aspects of the original project, any ideas that were never realised? Because of lack of money, or time perhaps?

JV   No, no. It was all done according to the standardised plan. We had to accommodate some changes, but mostly related to the terrain of the individual sites. Some of the sites were inclined, some were flat, some were small, irregular and so on.

    My understanding is that Niemeyer was the architect of the building and Darcy Ribeiro was the 'architect' of the actual programme, the curriculum. Did Niemeyer have any kind of input or interest in Darcy Ribeiro's ideas on education, or vice versa?

JV   I think that one influenced the other, yes. Darcy Ribeiro was very… He knew exactly what he wanted to do. He strongly believed that the educational system was the salvation of the country—that everything starts from education. He was always of the firm opinion that schools had to be run with a full-time schedule. Each environment had to accommodate every need in order to work well. So Niemeyer influenced him through architecture, designing projects in a way that really adapted his ideas about education.

So, the architecture and the curriculum were very closely connected?

JV   Yes. Oscar Niemeyer had already worked with Darcy Ribeiro when he built the University of Constantine, in Algeria. That university was made within a standardised system too, with an idea of mixing the students. Everything was influenced by Darcy Ribeiro in that project, regarding the creation and programming of the university.

Would you say that project had a big influence on the CIEPs project?

JV   Well no, because it is something else, it is really a different context. The Algerian university was a single project, whereas the design for the CIEPs had to be repeated five hundred times. And if Brizola had become president, the intention was to make ten thousand of them, across Brazil!

Oh, really? So there was an idea to build them everywhere?

JV   Unfortunately he never became president.

Would you have liked to have seen that happen?

JV   Yes, I think so. I agreed with him and with Darcy Ribeiro, that salvation for a country requires full-time education for all kids.

Obviously the CIEPs were only built in the state of Rio; do you think they would work as well in São Paulo, or in the North?

JV   I think that each state would have to re-think the project, considering climate issues, culture and so on. I think the element to repeat for sure would be simply the idea of being full-time and taking care of all the childrens' learning needs.

Chapter 5
The Pedagogical Adventure

The CIEP Ayrton Senna Da Silva and adjacent sports facility is connected to the Rocinha favela, via a Niemeyer-designed footbridge

Although the buildings were made from standard elements, the original CIEPs celebrated the unique cultural heritage of each individual site. The main vehicle for this was the cultural animation programme. Each CIEP employed a group of locally residing 'animators', bringing dance, music and other popular cultural expressions from the community into the school. This 'cultural animation' ensured that the standardised curriculum could value and build on local students' background and knowledge.

Under Leonel Brizola's government, CIEPs' teacher salaries were adjusted each semester in order to align with volatile inflation rates. They were also granted a gradual growth in their salaries according to the period for which they had been teaching. This made public school teaching a more attractive business than private. At the CIEP, daytime sessions would run from 7am to 5pm, catering for an average of 600 students; the evening session, largely serving older students, ran from 6pm to 10pm. The curriculum was split evenly between academic and extra-curricular activities, further modified through 'work projects' on salient topics such as hygiene and healthcare. Three square meals each day were carefully devised by a nutritionist in order to ensure a healthy, varied and balanced diet. Since health was one of the cornerstones of the CIEP project, a time slot was allocated for pupils to shower everyday, an amenity often not available at home. Each CIEP originally housed a health centre, serving not only students but also their families and community members. Staying clean and presentable formed a vital part of the CIEPs' curriculum, with a view to building students' self-esteem.

Students were issued with all the equipment necessary for school, from bathing soap to books and pencils. In addition, free travel was implemented in response to suggestions that many children could not attend school due to the cost; Brizola decreed free bus transport for uniform-wearing children, which later developed into an informal agreement with the bus companies.

The students of class #1501 and their teacher Vanete helped Aberrant Architecture with their research at the CIEP Tancredo de Neves

Darcy Ribeiro (d.1997) was one of the most respected intellectuals to emerge from Brazil in the twentieth century. A noted anthropologist, author and politician, Ribeiro supported Leonel Brizola as Vice Governor of Rio de Janeiro, during Brizolas's first term of office as State Governor. Ribeiro was fundamental in devising the CIEPs' pedagogical programme. However, Ribeiro's intellectual contribution and work within the fields of educational change began much earlier, making a more profound impact in Brazil than either of the other two instigators of the CIEPs.

Ribeiro's research, alongside fellow anthropologist Anísio Teixeira (d.1971), was seminal in its presentation of indigenous cultural values. In the 1960s, along with Teixiera, Ribeiro co-founded the Universidade de Brasília, even serving as its first rector. During his exile over Brazil's period of military dictatorship, his expertise took him across South America and beyond. The CIEPs are, in many ways, the urban realisation of the Park School, a radical model developed with Teixeira in the 1950s, in the state of Bahia. Ribeiro's belief in the 'civilising' effects of education influences the CIEPs' curriculum to this day.

The Teacher Speaks
Darcy Ribeiro, The Anthropologist

It is with great joy that we invite you to participate in the pedagogical adventure that is to reinvent, together, an honest and efficient public school. Let us, together, face the challenge of educating Brazilian children such as they are, from the concrete situation in which they find themselves.

The first two years of school act like a strainer, separating those who will be educated from those who will be rejected. It is mainly the poor children who fail, because schools tend to treat them as if they were on an equal footing with children from the most privileged backgrounds, making their academic success an almost impossible achievement.

A child who, since infancy, is encouraged to speak, is a privileged child considering the requirements of school. She talks to her parents, relatives and, in a way, also with television, with books, newspapers, with the theatre. She receives books as gifts, looks through magazines, sees people reading newspapers and writing letters. She tells people what she has done and what she wants to do. She has someone who listens and speaks even more than she does. Pencil, paper, eraser, typewriter, book shelves: these are things that have existed in her life, ever since she came to understand herself as a person. When it comes to school, even if they hide the 'road map' from her, she is bound to discover it anyway.

But what if a school could convey everything, note by note?

Maybe in that way, the poor child could participate in the story too. She might even invent other stories. Stories that speak of the things that she knows how to do: to climb, fall, run along and across streets; walk through the night, see in the dark and jump walls; to dance, talk, sing; to clean the house, cook and take care of her siblings; to fly kites, play jump-rope...

And what does this child need, in order to learn to read and write?

Firstly, to find out what writing has to do with speaking. And for this, she needs to talk. To feel that her speech is effective: that it serves for others to understand her, for her to speak about her life, to get to know the lives of others. It is through speaking that she will assert her own way of being, in relationship with those who are different from her.

At school, the child will learn how to speak in the way she is taught. But for this to happen, it is not necessary for her to be constantly corrected, only to end up feeling convinced that she cannot speak. She will need to learn the rules of what the school considers correct and beautiful as important conventions in our society, but not as truths or absolute values.

She will also need to learn how it is possible for language to reinvent the world: telling a story, for example. She will find that she can do this through drawing, writing, dancing, theatre—and that each of these various possible languages have their own wealth. And she will learn that through writing, she is able to capture what she says and pass it on.

With all this, she may engage with writing as something she understands and is able to use creatively, in service of herself and her community.

This is what the preparatory schooling is about: preparing the child for the process of becoming literate, as something that will enrich her life.

For this, other areas of knowledge need to be addressed: for example, logical, spatial and temporal reasoning. The child comes to school with reasoning developed in accordance with the references of their community. To master urban and academic cultures, she will need to learn how to think in the very language of these culture.

It is necessary to provide the child with situations where she, starting from her own sense of reason, develops a capacity for logical thinking, becoming able to discover comparisons that work with differences and similarities, to assess magnitudes and quantities and to build concepts.

Logical thinking, besides being useful to the development of language, will allow the knowledge of mathematics, of the sciences and so on. This knowledge is often provided by the school ignoring its logical connection, leaving with the child the need to memorise, using techniques such as visualisation, for example, rather than reasoning. This is the case, for example, of the concept of numbers. If at first such methods may be useful for the child to reach a right answer, it does not help much when she has to face new situations.

Pedagogy speaks much of the 'ability to transfer or generalise knowledge'. In fact, it is about allowing the student to discover those relationships that act as a kind of key to the production of knowledge. Contrary to what is usually thought, it is not by repetition and recording that the student gains an autonomy of knowledge.

Space and time are other areas where we need to calculate quantities and use measures. The child will need to make connections that allow her to calculate time in years, months and days or to assess the distance between one point and another.

With specific regard to written language skills, there are further spatial and temporal relationships that also need to be discovered by the child. For example, she needs to be able to locate herself in relation to the space of the paper, according to the conventions of our language: from left to right, top to bottom. Another example of a spatial-temporal relationship essential for literacy can be seen in successive ordering or construction, in order to establish a logical correspondence between the temporal sequence of speech and spatial sequence of writing.

When a phrase is said orally, words follow each other in time; when it is written, words follow each other in space (on a sheet of paper or the blackboard, for example). But to get all this, the child will need to learn to use the signs of time and space in language, locating situations she goes through closely and specifically. This location is formed beginning with the child's own ability to control and manage their physical actions. Coming and going, occupying different positions, delaying and anticipating actions; these are the bases of this knowledge. Talking about what she did before or after leaving school, for example, means that she will be thinking about her experiences, organising them in time. Similarly, to be located in space, within the references of our culture—up and down, left and right—one must experience it firstly, with the body. The down and the up could be experienced initially, for example, in the act of crouching under the table or standing on the chair.

At this stage of childhood, which lasts until eight or nine years of age, knowledge is gained with the entire body. The more the child can use her body, the richer her findings will be. For this to happen, it becomes important to explore the logic of the body: what it allows, what it says. How to produce some movements and the need to learn others. To learn, for example, the movements of writing.

Finally, an area that will be present throughout the project: socio-affective learning, that is, the part of work that addresses the emotional experience of attending school. This experience can be rich if you allow it.

In every moment it is essential that one's authority does not place the student's knowledge and her community in disrespect. In the proposed activities, she needs to be asked to draw from what she knows and contribute what she has to offer to the class. It is also important that she is able to bring to school what her relatives or friends have taught her outside the school, so she is able to trust that knowledge and teaching mean something different to everyone, and that everyone can be a teacher of something. Another important aspect relates to group relationships in the classroom. If you ask your students to perform only as individuals, only allowing individual activities, your class cannot become a group.

It is not enough to be seated together or even in a circle for a group to be created. It is important for children to have the opportunity to perform creatively, in situations where an interdependence between them is necessary. To work on stimulating and open tasks, so that they can arrive at a result built on the process of internal exchange. That is to say, a unified group can be produced as such, as long as there are favourable conditions.

On the other hand, it is precisely in this world of known and unknown experiences that you and the kids can connect, in a kind of alliance. Because the experience with this class will be—at first—an experience of the unknown, also for you. Each class is a lesson, and every experience is unique and new. Especially when it comes to children. You and they have a lot to learn together. And so do we, along with you.

The Special Education Programme, in which you now participate, is designed to render possible the honest and efficient public school that we mentioned at the beginning of our conversation. It holds, as one of its strongest principles, the belief that improving the quality of education in literacy classes is the first and foremost challenge to build a school that meets the needs of the popular clientele. On the success of literacy rests the continuity of the whole educational process.

We believe that the large rate of failures in literacy is largely due to the inadequacy with which the public schools deal with most children, but also the lack of teaching materials, which are as necessary as meals. It is equally due to the lack of support experienced by teachers, who face the challenge of literacy work without adequate training. It is this support that we intend to give you, as a literacy teacher, in the form of educational materials that will help you in your day-to-day activities in the classroom and also by creating space for your in-service training.

The material we present to you is not intended to replace you, but to assist you in the classroom. You will see that it is not just a package with suggestions for activities and exercises for children; it is directed both to the child and to you. Just as the children's materials should help them in their task of learning, your materials are designed to help you in the task of teaching.

To facilitate your work in the classroom, the material will arrive in your hands in successive deliveries, made throughout the year. This one is the first. With the other ones you will also receive a letter, in which we will try to provide ideas to use the material with your students; it will also clarify the goals implicit in the suggested exercises and activities, and their relevance to the teaching of literacy.

And remember: every child can learn. The school is responsible for ensuring the conditions needed for success, and not to punish her for not yet knowing that which no one has taught her.

Text continues on page 118

Life in the CIEPs—Health and Wellbeing

Health was vital to the CIEP project; time was allocated for bathing (1), a luxury for the many children who did not have showers at home. Keeping themselves and their uniforms in clean and good condition formed part of the curriculum. Each CIEP hosted a dental facility (2), staffed twice a week by a qualified dentist, as well as a Medical Centre (3) serving students, families and community members. Besides routine clinical services, the Centre offered eye care, nutritional advice and health education, so that each person was able to spread knowledge within the community. Materials in the Medical Centre were standardised to rationalise costs. Every student and employee went through a medical exam when admitted into the school. Small residential blocks on the roof (4) housed certain students during the week, who would return to their family homes at the weekend. In contrast to the school buildings,

the rooftop residential quarters were small and domestically proportioned. At break-time, the entire school becomes a giant playground, with students sliding down the ramps (5) and playing in the multitude of spaces. Transport to school on the city buses (6) was free for children in school uniforms. Without this service, many children would not have been able to afford the travel to and from school. The CIEPs provided the children with three meals a day and other supplements, carefully designed by a nutritionist to ensure a balanced diet (7). Processed foods were replaced with produce sourced from local markets. Decentralising food supplies enabled unprecedented levels of trade between small businesses and the state, reducing costs by over 40%. A daily milk distribution system, favouring schools and the rural producer simultaneously, was also implemented.

Life in the CIEPs—A Typical Day, Part 1

One radical proposal of the CIEPs was the offer of integral 'full-time' education; as a facility, the CIEPs were open from morning to night. Students could spend the whole day at the CIEP (1) where the curriculum was split evenly between academic and extra-curricular activities. Each school developed pedagogic reference books (2) taking into consideration individual teaching experiences. Students had more opportunity to express their ideas orally (3), which helped to enhance their self-esteem and confidence. Traditional academic subjects were replaced with an integrated curriculum (4); skills were not taught independently, but instead relationships (between mathematics and language, for example) were pointed out whenever possible. Originally, classrooms were designed with half-height walls, which meant that students and teachers had to speak

quietly (5). If appropriate voice education was implemented, noise interference would improve. This is an example of how the CIEPs' architecture was intrinsically tied to the pedagogical project. Half-walls also ensured that all interior spaces were cross-ventilated, and allowed the central corridor to function as an exhibition space (6). The curriculum was enhanced by 'work projects' (7), special exercises where teachers and other professionals, such as health officials and cultural animators, worked together to combat issues like head lice. Schools plagued by head lice would often find parents relying on traditional remedies passed from generation to generation—using toothpaste or oil for example, which rarely removed the lice. Work Projects shared recipes for homemade coconut shampoo for de-lousing (8) which could easily be made by the childrens' parents at home.

Life in the CIEPs—A Typical Day, Part 2

Every CIEP had a group of 'cultural animators' (9) whose purpose was to bring artistic expressions from the students' local communities into the school. Dancers (10), who had developed their talents outside the school, for example, shared skills with the children. Samba is an integral part of many local communities; percussion classes were often added to the curriculum (11). Instruments included caixas, tamborins, agogô bells, surdos, ganzás, cuícas, timbas and pandeiros (12). Through activities like these, the culture of marginalised students was accepted and incorporated into the school. Activities such as capoeira (13) acted as stepping stones to the teaching of high-order skills necessary for urbane lifestyles. Parental and community involvement at the CIEPs was promoted through weekend leisure activities. Parties, exhibitions or events celebrated important dates, linking to a cultural or communal celebrations such as a weddings (14). Regular training and staff meetings between principals, pedagogical coordinators, pastoral counsellors, and teachers were crucial. To deliver an effective integrated curriculum, CIEP teachers often met (15) to plan lessons across various subject areas. At least once a week after the training sessions, teachers planned their lessons together; all problems were discussed and strategies adopted by a vote of teachers. CIEPs' school members made concerted efforts to involve the broader community in the school's activities and programme. The CIEPs called for at least two meetings per semester between teachers and parents (16). Teachers were also encouraged to work within the community to become more familiar with the students' reality.

Speaking to Teachers: Our Students

The fundamental requirement for every teacher should be to take a socially responsible approach in exercising his important professional mission, as a teacher of Brazilian children, as they are the overwhelming majority. A teacher is measured by the number of children in need that he inspires, improves and elevates, and not by the performance of bright students who would progress equally with or without his assistance.

To adequately serve a student body from more popular origins, the first skill that has to be developed relates to spoken language. One must learn to listen and discern well what the child did before coming to school. First, she needs to become familiar with the language of the teacher, sometimes very different from what she hears and speaks at home, and much closer to what she will find in written language. She must also be carefully trained to discern in what is heard, the indispensable minutiae required in writing and reading, which have, however, no significance to the spoken language. Above all, your student needs to speak. To speak spontaneously, saying things, telling stories, commenting on events, because their ability to communicate fluently is the basis of the power of reasoning that she should develop.

In the field of language, care must firstly be taken not to frustrate students. Many teachers inhibit—sometimes crushing for life—the student's predisposition to learn by being overzealous. We must remember that the language of the teacher, although it corresponds more closely to a classical standard, is the speech of the minority. Popular children do not know this speech. They know the language spoken in their homes and neighbourhoods, which is the way of speaking for most Brazilians.

That is why we can only introduce the student progressively and slowly to the classical standard known as cultural or academic language. However, the way to do it is not with ceaseless corrections of pronunciation, verb tenses, gender, number or degree. That is, not the method of punishing the child of popular origin for being as she is, while rewarding the boy who—coming from the same social circle as the teacher—speaks the only language he knows as his own.

The way to get a child to master scholarly language is to familiarise her with the right words and pauses, through patient explanations and through speech of the teacher, which each student will eventually copy. In this way she is enabled, gradually, to master the necessary elements of reading and writing, eventually discovering another type of speech and other levels of understanding.

A prerequisite for any of this to occur is that the student develops a degree of trust, appreciation and self-respect. This is only feasible in an environment where there is respect for people of your type, for your family, for your social class. Only where the popular student feels free to talk, inquire, question, vindicate, can he or she learn.

Frustrated at the first plane of communication, she takes refuge in silence or fear. Outwardly she is miserable: queen of the street, but at school a shy girl who fails in academic life, though she exhibits the highest qualifications for practical life. In some cases, she takes the path of delinquency, unable to enter the world of people who speak and dress beautifully. The teacher cannot ignore or forget that he represents a key role in a child's emotional development. He is able to help the child grow through an acceptance and recognition of her own identity, being proud of herself.

It is important to divide time at school into periods of work and rest, requiring neither more nor less than what each student can give. It is necessary to avoid unnecessary effort. No use in insisting on activities that the student has already mastered well, turning repetition in scarcely bearable routine. Finally, it is essential to always keep evaluating the performance of each student, mainly through close observation.

The formation of each teacher must include a detailed knowledge of the biological and mental development of the students, and of their progressive integration in social life through learning that, in complex societies, is achieved through school education.

It is with this knowledge, accumulated over centuries, but most especially in recent decades, that thinkers and scientists have developed what we now call pedagogy—the science and art of teaching.

But not even all knowledge in the world is enough to make you into an effective teacher, if you do not develop, simultaneously, a real sympathy for your students. Therefore it is essential that you grow a high sensitivity to the problems and needs of each of them. Only this sympathy and sensitivity will enable you to motivate them to make great efforts to progress in education. That is why it is said that education requires both competence and love. It is important to be well-equipped, but wise as you may be, you will need to keep an open mind and heart, to learn more and better express sympathy. There is always more to learn in the arts of listening, living and above all working. But only those who are willing to revise their assumptions are able to learn. Anísio Teixeira often repeated that he had no commitment to his ideas, meaning that his commitment was to the search for truth and understanding. There is always more to learn. There is also always more love to give and receive, if we have open minds and open hearts.

Originally published in 'O Livro Dos Cieps', (Bloch Editores S.A, 1986), a book intended to act as a manual for the CIEPs' initiative.

Overleaf: Learning was split evenly between the curriculum and extra-curricular activities like art, music, dance and sports—all designed to be closely integrated. This was ensured with continual exchange between classroom and other teachers.
Each CIEP had a team of cultural animators who helped create bonds between community and school. Cultural animation ensured that local community life and culture was incorporated into the school's daily routine. They did this by selecting discussion themes, designing a range of activities to entertain and stimulate the children. Typically, around 600 students would attend a CIEP in the day and 400 in the evening. One of the CIEPs after-hours initiatives was known as the Juvenile Educational Program, which aimed to provide specific opportunities for young people who had already exceeded the mandatory educational age, but who were still illiterate. These young people, marginalised in a society where literacy is mandatory, were offered classes in regular subjects whilst also being encouraged to share their experiences. Creating and developing each young person's individual identity was seen as vitally important. Due to the challenging social circumstances of their upbringing, many young people did not see themselves as fully rounded people or even deserving of life.
Teaching classes in citizenship was seen as a vitally important instrument. These citizenship classes began by making each student aware of themselves as an individual person, existing in time and space, within the physical world. The hope was that by being conscious of their own environment, each young person might evolve a deeper understanding of themselves as an individual, as a member of the community, as well as developing a more critical view of society and the wider world.

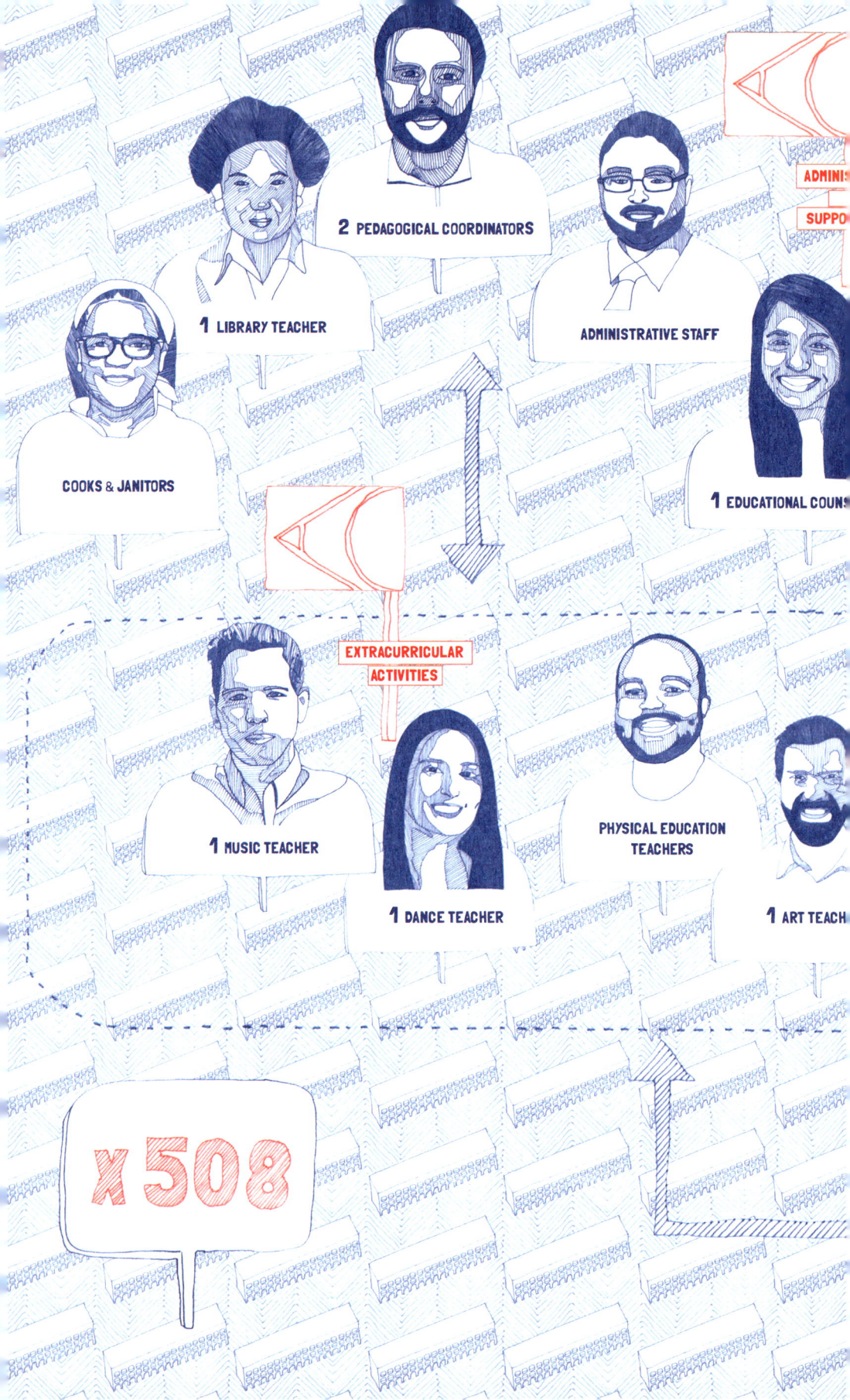

Chapter 6
The School Is Yours

Break time: taking a time-out on the ping-pong tables at the playground of the CIEP Presidente Tancredo Neves in Catete

Our first visit to a CIEP school took us to the Presidente Tancredo Neves, in Catete—appropriately enough, the first full CIEP scheme ever to be constructed in Rio's South Zone, in 1985. At break-time, the school resembled a giant playground, with students sliding down the ramps and playing under the large covered arcade. Ribeiro and Niemeyer had intended for children to be able to run around the CIEPs large open spaces freely, in contrast to the small dark alleys of the favela.

We visited the octagonal library building, which is separated from the main block in order to receive special classes as well as members of the wider community. The library acts as a forum space for discussions, as well as supporting various clubs and cultural activities.

CIEP Tancredo Neves is one of the few schools to retain the small residential blocks on the roof—one for twelve boys and another which can accommodate twelve girls. These little houses serve those children whose parents are unable to look after them during the week; at the weekends they are usually sent home, so as not to break family bonds. These days, the residential scheme runs sporadically, at just a handful of the CIEPs.

The large outdoor sports court provides students with a large shaded space to play games, practice capoeira, stage concerts, or even host parties. Niemeyer actually called this court the Multipurpose Room, imagining it as a type of public square—one of the most important spaces for integrating the CIEP with the community.

A beautiful water tower completes the CIEP Tancredo Neves' full kit of standardised parts.

We asked students to draw what they liked about their school. Most popular by far were the sports court and the library buildings: a big thumbs-up for Ribeiro's and Niemeyer's original vision, awarded from the most important people at the school.

A student from class #1501 draws his favourite part of CIEP Presidente Tancredo Neves, the first of the CIEP buildings

Carmen Silvia Menna Barreto is a lawyer with more than twenty years of experience in civil litigation; she has been teaching in the city of Rio for thirty years. As a teacher, she worked for ten years in the CIEP Presidente Tancredo Neves in the education programme for young people and adults, and at the Paulo Freire Institute for teacher training. She currently works in the Management of Administration and Human Resources of SMERJ. (Municipal Secretary of Education for Rio de Janeiro).

Luís Fernando Maciel Balata is a lawyer based in Rio de Janeiro, and born in São Luís in the northeast of Brazil. He held a public office during the second government of Governor Leonel Brizola. He was a member of the Commission for Human Rights and the Ethics and Discipline Tribunal of the Lawyers Association of Brazil. Currently he is a lawyer dedicated to civil and family law, and is also engaged in activities linked to social and political issues.

We met Carmen and Fernando together on Sunday 1 April, 2012, at the Cobal do Humaíta market, designed in 1971 by Alcides Horácio de Azevedo. Over a coffee, we discussed the CIEPs' evolution from inception to present day.

A Conversation with Carmen Silvia Barretto and Fernando Balata
   The Teacher and The Lawyer

   Tell us about your role in the CIEPs project.
CB   In 1986, I passed my professional teaching exams in the city of Rio de Janeiro. A friend who knew the director of the CIEP Tancredo Neves asked me to work there. It was a special programme where you taught for 40 hours each week. So in 1987, I started on this schedule: I would start at 7:15am and leave at 5pm. I taught a literacy class.
   What are your initial thoughts regarding the CIEPs project?
CB   Well, it was and still is a wonderful project. From a social point of view it was always impressive, and today I think it is great from the educational point of view too, even more than before. Nowadays it is the opposite, now teachers in Brazil must have a Bachelor's degree, as well as the technical diploma. The teachers arrive better prepared nowadays, but back then even if you left the Teacher Training Course and started at a CIEP, you would learn there. The staff felt directly connected to Professor Darcy Ribeiro: he would send us a kit, like a series of notebooks, each subject with a different colour. If my classroom had twenty pupils, I would receive twenty kits—and there would be a weekly visit from a senior teacher who would provide guidance for us. From this point of view, I am a better teacher today for being part of this project.
   What were the criticisms towards the initial programme, at the time—if there were any?
CB   Perhaps that the best part of the solution was also part of the problem. This idea of receiving everything as a pre-defined system meant that you could not develop it too much. And if your pupils had a question beyond the given curriculum, then you wouldn't really know how to assist. It was not too much of an open discussion: 'Do this!' Perhaps that was the only criticism. The physical space was wonderful, the food was great, the atmosphere was good, the directors were very well prepared—my director, a former student of Darcy Ribeiro, is still a professor of anthropology at *Universidade Federal Fluminense*, one of the four state universities of Rio de Janeiro.
   And when do you think there was a major change from the situation that you have just described?
CB   Certainly at the end of Brizola's government, right? At the end of Brizola's second term. The management of the CIEPs was divided at that time between the authorities of the City of Rio de Janeiro, and the state of Rio de Janeiro. The CIEPs outside the city were taken by the state network—but the state governor, Moreira Franco, did not have a political interest in maintaining a project of his political rivals, Brizola and Ribeiro. I think that's when the big change happened.
   Some people said that the existing public schools at that time could have been redesigned, instead of putting money into designing and building these new schools. What's your opinion about this?
CB   I think that's nonsense. That's nonsense, because at the beginning, the main idea was about the opportunity to take children off the street full-time. Taking a child off the street means protecting them from a certain kind of community—so that the child does not get involved with drug trafficking for example, selling or using, or stealing. The CIEPs really did help with that. Catete, for example, was a neighbourhood that you couldn't walk through without someone stealing your wallet and having that CIEP really improved safety there. But this silliness of 'one way or the other'—that's nonsense. Of course, there are mothers who want half-time schooling for their children, and there are children who can't stand staying inside a CIEP all day. Some children adapt to schools which

offer a half-day programme, and others prefer a full-time programme. It's for a more independent type of child really.

> **What were the programme's key successes and failures?**

CB   Things that we might have changed, you mean? Because the initial curriculum was really well planned. The only negative point in the early days would have been the silliness of recruiting absolute beginner teachers without any experience—like me at the time. We would receive the curriculum already formatted and then would not feel as though we had any flexibility, to take a turn if there was any doubt. The curriculum was tight, very tight.

> **The CIEPs reformed the conventional idea of separate disciplines, and the activities were designed to encourage the pupils to make connections between the different subjects. Can you recall an example of this?**

CB   Yes, I can. For example, through the description of a maths exercise, you can find out if the student knows Portuguese. If he understands the description of the task, it is because he understands the language, so it shows some knowledge of Portuguese. So now we've got Portuguese and maths. If that exercise talks about kilograms or measuring units, it connects through to science too, because he will also get to learn about things you use in physics. And so it goes... It's the integration of all of the subjects.

> **And that depends on the teachers, so that they were able to identify these connections…**

CB   Exactly. Because during our diploma training courses, the subjects were clearly divided. You would study teaching techniques for maths, in order to teach maths. Or techniques for Portuguese, or for social studies. Then when you entered a project like the CIEPs, you would re-train for a whole month so that you could adapt what you knew into an integrated way of teaching.

> **Extra-curricular activities were also designed to be joined up to the core curriculum, right, with the traditional subjects?**

CB   Yes! It was the first time I saw students going to museums, for example... Children would not leave public school for outings before—except maybe only to the zoo. But during the CIEPs programme, they started going to CCBB *(Centro Cultural Banco do Brasil)*, they started going to the *France-Brazil House*, they would go see exhibitions. Even without knowing too much about art or anything... The teacher would search for an artist. And then they could go, look at the work, let's say it was serigraphy or silk-screening; the teacher would explain to the pupils what serigraphy is…

> **Can you talk a little about the relationship between the school curriculum and the social context of the pupils? Socially or culturally, in terms of folklore or traditions… Were there any concerns or stories related to these differences?**

CB   There was one… It was super interesting. The philosophy for Darcy was that the school belonged to the pupil, not the teacher. So at the beginning of the school year, we had to put posters around the school saying, 'The school is yours', you know what I mean? The teacher would even feel a little threatened. As a teacher, you did not have any right, inside the school.
If a pupil wrote an essay, it didn't really matter if the essay was wrong. You had to evaluate what he had done and then you would try to improve it with him as much as you could. You could not say 'You're missing the "F" here and the "L" there', nothing that could get his self-esteem down. I remember one time when I was getting the pupils to stand in a row and Darcy himself was visiting; he would visit this school weekly. But then

my pupils broke out of their rows and I, poor me at 18 years old, started running after them, my sandals fell apart… Then he called me over, 'Come here, sweetie, come here, come here. Look, when they break out you don't go running like this, ok. You stay put in your place and they will run to you.' *(Laughs).* And I was really embarrassed, all over the place, you know…

FB   But there is something more to this question. In reality the CIEPs, the pedagogical approach, was based on the ideas of *Paulo Freire*. He made exactly this connection, this interaction between learning and the social reality of students, do you see what I mean? And that was one of the ideas and reasons for resistance against the project. Paulo Freire's methodology was applied in the formulation of the CIEPs project.

Everyone knows Paulo Freire as a figure who was cursed by the military dictatorship, imprisoned and then exiled. When Brizola arrived and took command of Rio de Janeiro's government, and started to implement this educational project, Freire's return was still very recent. In the key part of the public administration there were still many people who were directly linked to the military dictatorship, who resisted these changes. There was this great resistance because of that, just that. The pedagogical basis of the CIEPs was really linked to social and community aspects, right, the reality of the pupils themselves. What stood out most about the project at that time was this.

> Giving more importance to the students and to their local culture…

CB   Exactly.

> What about the cultural animation programme? What was it exactly, how did it work, if you have any examples…

CB   Yes, there is an example. The cultural animation project was not delivered by municipal teachers; these were people contracted by the Cultural Secretary, not the Education Secretary. The programme was usually very theatrical, always using the idea of representation. In fact, they would do little plays with us, with teachers presenting to the pupils. They did weekly lessons with the students, and a lot of them involved working with the body. I found some of the exercises interesting, like the pushing-falling one… Where you let me push you backwards so someone else will catch you, you know? Of course, the pupils would not trust it. Imagine, for a child who lives in the favela to trust someone to push them backwards and that they would be caught! It was incredible.

> In your opinion then, was the cultural animation programme a successful idea?

CB   Yes, I think so, I think so. It involved some art in the sense of performance; I think if there was only one kind of art that the students could really understand, it was this one.

> And why do you think it was deactivated, this project?

CB   Cultural animation is still present in the programme for young people and for adult education. Every Friday there is a class—mostly theatre, I have never seen painting, I've only seen theatre. But the programme was a product between the secretaries for culture and education, because the cultural animators were not education staff. They normally didn't have a particularly high level of education, right? The cultural animation staff did not have diplomas, they had talent.

> How about the Social Parent programme—how did that idea come about? Was that part of the original project?

CB   Yes, it's original. The original idea was that someone local, like a firefighter—or if I'm not mistaken, it was two members of the community, a social mum and a social dad, who would live in the school, to take care of twelve boys on one side and twelve girls on the other. And those 'parents' would live there with the children. At the beginning it was like this. You did visit the little houses, right?

>> We did, we went upstairs to the roof.

CB And is it still all tidy?

>> Yes, but only the boys' house is accessible. The girls' house is closed, I am not sure why. There were nine boys living there, with the capacity for twelve as you said. The director of the project, Vera is her name, said that the only criterion for the Social Parent is that it must be someone who already works at the CIEP and is part of the community. So, it could be, for example, the cook, or… Could it be a teacher?

CB No, it can't be a teacher. Otherwise, they would all be living there! *(Laughter)*

>> But it has to be someone who is working there already, right, or living in the community, like you said. Here, we met Silvestre.

CB Yes, Silvestre has worked with me since 1986—we have grown old together, Silvestre and I.

>> But the Social Parent programme doesn't exist at all the CIEPs anymore, right? What happened?

CB Yes, because we had some serious problems of sexual abuse, you know? There were pregnancies and the Public Ministry had to act, so now the Social Care Secretary follows the programme very closely under instruction of the Special Court for Children and Adolescents.
It's funny—these CIEP residences actually support the Special Court for Children and Adolescents quite a lot. For example, take the street kids who commit some kind of crime—until he or she is trialled by the court, they put him or her in a CIEP residence. Or when a mum or dad fails to pick their child up from other schools in the area, they call the social worker, who very often takes the child to a CIEP residence to sleep because the parents didn't pick them up. So the residence actually services the requirements of the Special Court.

>> Yes. I thought it was interesting, that not all of the children living there, necessarily attend the CIEP school.

CB No, no. There are children who stay there on a temporary basis, that's a separate thing. But the ones who live there also study there. Now, if there is someone from another school who needs to sleep there because the judge sent him or her, then they do. It has created a complex integration of work, between the social worker, the judge and the person responsible for the residence. It's a failure of justice, right…

>> The CIEPs were clearly an innovative programme that offered a way out from the traditional concepts, of the traditional relationship between teachers and parents. In your opinion, how did this shift in the relationship happen? How did it happen and how long did it take?

CB The project remains innovative, even though historically speaking, the CIEPs' curriculum ran for no time at all. For education, this time period of several years is not that significant, right. Only now are we starting to bear fruit from this project. But it remains innovative.
In Brazil… This social class I'm describing—who knows what classification it is!—does not seem to value education. A parent from this social class might not worry too much about the formal education of his child, they do not have these expectations—they mainly appreciate the project because the child can stay there safely all day. Because they have the encouragement of the teachers, the children are able to be themselves —to realise their potential—in school. But in their homes there is no encouragement, there still isn't. In fact some of the parents used to say: 'Ah, in my family everyone is stupid, they are not going to learn anything anyway…'

>**Okay, let me ask you something else. Recently, we saw a news report about a campaign to bring back the idea of a full-time school, based on the original CIEPs idea. What's your opinion on that?**

CB   I do know about the campaign; the secretary Claudia Costin stated that there are about 150 schools which have adopted a seven-hour shift. In fact, now most public placements for teachers are only for full-time programmes. I think that soon all schools, or at least the municipal ones in Rio de Janeiro, will be full-time.

>**Do you think this is a return to the original ideas of the CIEPs or is it different?**

CB   It is an attempt, but nothing will ever be as fantastic as the original project was. If you build the appropriate space... I'll give you a simple example: the CIEPs' building has a reading room, this round thing here, look. Then here, you can do everything, theatre, film, reading circles... Try and do these things inside a little room, in a traditional school, you can't. It is not the appropriate space or environment: there are no acoustics, no light, no place for the children to sit on the floor, no bathroom...

>**So, in this sense, you think that the architecture of the CIEP really does incorporate all those ideas from the curriculum?**

CB   It's fundamental, I think it's fundamental. A full-time school is never going to function as well as a CIEP does without this building. It won't.

>**Could you imagine a new generation of CIEPs being built—a CIEPs 2.0, if you like? And if you can imagine it, what would you change or keep from the original project?**

CB   In terms of the architecture, I would bring back the half-wall—it is impossible to work in so much heat, especially as the windows do not open! The half-wall allows the circulation of air, at least. And I would also digitise everything, including a lot more of the learning. A CIEP like the one you visited in Tancredo Neves has a computer lab with just ten or twelve computers, between hundreds of students.

>**The CIEPs programme was clearly an innovative school project for its time... But it seems that it was entirely imposed by government and other qualified people. You might say that although the programme is socially concerned and collaborative, in reality it did not take into consideration the wishes of the community; it appears to be a top-down vision. How do you think the project was conceived, both the architecture and the curriculum?**

CB   In Brazil, this idea of 'top down' education does not make sense, because there are very few means for education at a 'bottom-up' level. It was simply about having a place to educate your children. It was more important to give them showers, physical education, a useful level of qualification and food, within a full time schedule. That answered the needs of the community, that's what mattered more than the details of the curriculum. In fact, often the parents themselves could not read.

>**Staying on this topic, another question. Was there a feeling from the local community that the schools were actually too sophisticated, somehow too much? Perhaps a feeling they could not immediately relate to them, that they did not 'get' the project?**

CB   No. The project was very well disseminated. More than that, everything that you give to the people raises their expectations, and then they think it is their right. Some people might appreciate it, but for others it's more like, 'This is my right; you did nothing more than what you should be doing.' For many people, there isn't an understanding of this social vision, only the 'right' for the child to be educated.

FB With regards to your question, what happened was the following: it's true, when the project was implemented it caused a massive impact on the communities because, as you understand, it was an imposing project with regards to its architecture. In the middle of extremely deprived communities, poorly urbanised. It was such a progressive education plan, keeping the child for the entire day in school. And then giving them an environment of comfort and security that in reality, the children did not have in their immediate surroundings—this caused a 'love affair' with the CIEPs and a resistance at the same time, you see? But afterwards, with more interaction—even because of the cultural animation, which also tried to make those links—when there was a constant interaction between the parents, the children and the teachers of the CIEPs and the use of the CIEPs for leisure activities…

Yes. On weekends, students in the region could go to the pool, as some of the CIEPs had a swimming pool, or use the multipurpose courts. And the children could take their parents with them, you know? So this interaction began and then the CIEPs really became a loved project.

CB It was a leisure space where previously there was nothing. I mean, on the side of Brasil Avenue, you had a deprived community. That sports court was a great leisure space: parents would go there and play football, or have a barbecue inside—how great!

> **Well, it's a wonderful space, isn't it?**

CB Even weddings, sometimes, of former pupils. The *CIEPs Tancredo Neves* has even had two or three weddings.

> **But going back to the top-down, bottom-up discussion… Do you think it is necessary, in order to realise such a broad social intention, that you give the project over to a community?**

CB If people have more of a social vision, a degree of understanding, a degree of interest… I think this would be interesting if it was in a mixed school—if in this school there was both rich and poor pupils, like in the public schools. At the CIEPs, most of the parents earn so little that they cannot access even a minimum level of culture. Minimum salaries are shameful, and corruption is so widespread, so that you are grateful to leave your kids in any school and go to work as a cleaner, great.

So that you get a proper idea, 60% of my pupils at the time had fathers in jail. 60%, almost two thirds. That's a very high percentage. So can you imagine, how the mothers managed? Do you think these mothers were in any condition to know whether the curriculum was good or to even have an opinion about it? If you set up a meeting, she could probably not even get there, because she would be on endless cleaning jobs. It is a social problem really, which makes it difficult for families to get involved in the quality of education for their children.

> **Don't you think that with projects of this stature, like the implementation of a public schools programme, that they should be done with a greater level of consensus, across parties? To avoid wasting money during one political term, only to have it changed with the next regime? Clearly that was detrimental to the project's success.**

CB Look, I think every educational project should be non-partisan. Because education concerns everyone, everyone. So it should be non-partisan. But it is important to understand that the project is not over. There was a decline with Brizola's death, when Moreira Franco took power—but this does not change things. Currently, the education secretary Claudia Costin is a very well-prepared person. She is not a teacher, she is an administrative person, which is great. I think putting someone in education who is a good administrator was a very smart move, she sees it with different eyes.

Ok, just one more question. The CIEPs programme had a lot of freedom; at the beginning it was autonomous from the existing state and municipal bureaucracies. It was coordinated by the Education Coordinating Commission, which consisted of just three members: the Education Secretary, the dean of one of Rio's state universities and the deputy-governor. But what were the reasons for that?

CB   I believe it was a budgetary requirement; the project had a specific budget, so they needed to create a committee to manage it, you see? It required various materials, specific food, special equipments, for example. At the start of the year the CIEPs would receive material that other schools in the region would not get, and the money for this had to come from somewhere. Perhaps that's why there was a need for the existence of a managing committee.

Do you know if the committee still exists?

CB   No, not anymore. But I work in the management department now: I manage human resources and I oversee fifteen schools. One of them is CIEP Bento Rubião. My colleague oversees another fifteen schools, and CIEP Tancredo Neves is one of those. It is all properly allocated.

Okay so one final question: the architect Oscar Niemeyer worked in a number of projects of a social nature, concerned with social welfare. But he also says, in his autobiography, that he had the feeling with these projects—including the CIEPs—that he was conspiring with manipulative and paternalistic objectives. That such projects might represent a political agenda which aimed to fool the working classes, the poorest classes. How do you think the CIEPs project worked in relation to these ideas?

CB   I think this is completely unfair. You see, I think the CIEPs was the most socially minded and coolest thing he did. Not what he built in Minas Gerais, not even Brasília… To me, in my opinion, this is the coolest thing he did, which still stands today.

Thank you very much.

CB   You're welcome, darlings.

Overleaf: The covered arcade between the medical centre, formerly part of the school, and the canteen, at CIEP Presidente Tancredo Neves

Renata Carneiro Moura is Adjunct Director of Pedagogy at CIEP Presidente Tancredo Neves. She has been working at the school for several years, first as a teacher and then, elected by peers, as an adjunct director—thereby taking on more responsibility for the school operations and physical condition.

Having imbibed the principles and narrative of the original project, it made sense to confront the reality of the CIEPs' ongoing operations. Visiting examples of the CIEPs several decades after their establishment allowed us but a snapshot, but Renata, students and staff shared with us their intimate and critical experiences of the CIEPs as users.

We visited the Tancredo Neves school just before lunchtime on Friday 30 March, 2012, when the whole site seemed to be one giant playground, with children sliding down bannisters, running around the wide ramps and the open sports court. After showing us the building's original plans and drawings in the staff room, Renata took us on a detailed tour of the school, pointing out problems, changes and adaptations made to the building.

A Conversation with Renata Carneiro
> The Director

RC   This is not original, we used to have these half-height walls.
> **Oh, so these were the half-walls here?**

RC   Yes. From here, every room was just half-walls. Up to here, yes… Then we had to put in this partition, something acoustic…
> **Probably to absorb the sound, right?**

RC   Yes. To make it a little bit quieter. It was way too noisy, way too noisy. But some of them are falling already… *(laughs)*
> **When were the half-walls filled in and refurbished?**

RC   Four years ago. They were open before that.
> **Did you have to get permission for that? For modifying the design?**

RC   Yes. This is the only modification we were permitted to make… Here is our bathroom. *(Sighs)* What are children doing in here, this is the 'Aunties' bathroom..
> **This is for the students, is it?**

RC   No, for us, *(laughter)*. We're in the process of adapting to new management, although I have worked here for five years. The previous director retired, so we had to go through the whole process of applying to be elected to a directing position. So now we have a new group: Deise, Maria Augusta and myself, we have been sharing the directorship at this CIEP for just over a month.
> **So who elected you?**

RC   The whole community. Students, parents and the teachers, yes.
> **Were there rival candidates?**

RC   Yes! We had two groups. Every two years we have elections for a new group.
> **Ok, but if you don't get elected, do you get given another job or…**

RC   Yes, we would just remain as regular teachers. This is our office. And this part also had a half-wall, but we had to close it here for security after we had some computers stolen some years ago… We have just two classrooms with computers.

Enters a classroom and speaks to the kids

Excuse me everyone! Look, I am going to tell you something, just a minute! This 'uncle' came from London, all the way from England to see our CIEP, look how fancy! He came to see how a classroom is here in Brazil, a really well-behaved and beautiful one, so I came to show you guys. You know how to speak English, you have English lessons! What do you say?

KIDS   Hello!
> **Hello!**

RC   We had the half-wall here too. But it's the same, how can I say, the same pattern or layout as before.
> **And did the half-walls have built in shelves, like this one?**

RC   Uh yes… I think that it was here before the refurbishment.
> **Good bye!**

RC   Good bye, you know how to say it!

KIDS   Good bye!

RC   They have only been having English classes since the middle of the last year. This is a video room and then downstairs we have a theatre, which we added during the refurbishment. And this is the teachers' room, with a lot of textbooks. Nowadays we don't use these so much; City Hall produces a booklet. Over there, there are more didactic books for adult learning in the evening.

The School Is Yours

What time do the children leave school?

RC   Half past four in the afternoon, and then at six in the evening we begin with the adults. Here we have all the student files and archives, and this is the kindergarten area. At this time, the children are about to leave. Now, one thing that you will notice: they are very, very dirty! Because we have a lot of places for them to play....

It's the heat as well, isn't it…

RC   There is the heat. Before we had a routine of giving them showers here, to avoid sending them home dirty. But well, it must be more than ten or fifteen years since that was stopped.

Is this the original ceiling? And then you added this cladding or lining wall here? Why was it added?

RC   Because the original grey made the room very dark and it's ugly too, very ugly. And we had a problem with this ceiling because when it rains, we have leaks. But it's interesting to see what was there before, right?

I like it! It's… Serious. A very serious grey. It's very architectural. But it's probably not very nice for a school.

RC   Not nice at all... So we are trying to see how we can replace these here, these panels. Because they are old and specially designed parts, they don't sell them anymore, it looks like we will have to get them remade. We're trying to figure it out. The lamps are hard to find too. Because they are unique, the company that made them used these special fittings and we just can't find them, you see?

Why didn't people just paint the original ceiling, just paint it white?

RC   I don't know, ha ha ha. Good question. I don't know.

Perhaps because of the sound, as well. This new material is insulating, it has holes to absorb the sound.

RC   It's much much quieter than it was before. Let me see if I can show you something that was not original. Actually it could all be painted, now that you mention it. I would love to colour the CIEP, I think it's really depressing to have this dirty white. I wanted to use a happier colour, you know?

So when you get elected, do you have something like a discretionary budget to use for improvements like this?

RC   No, no, only dreams! We have the ideas, we have a project, but we are not certain that it will be put into action...

Who would you need to get approval from?

RC   The municipal government. We get a budget to spend on durable goods and soft goods, services. We have some emergency funds to buy things and then we have to forget other plans... This is the second floor. Here we have most of the classrooms. In some cases two teachers split the same classroom.

But do you still have extra-curricular activities?

RC   It's not like it was in the original plan. In the original schedule, the entire afternoon was for other activities, but this is no longer the case.

We saw a newspaper report recently, which talked about your work here at Tancredo Neves.

RC   Oh you've seen it? That was my classroom. I didn't want it to seem like promotion, I only did it to talk about the CIEPs—because I am a big Brizola fan, a very big fan, you know? Not everyone is, but I am. I am a particularly strong defendant of the CIEPs idea—but his original idea, which has been largely subverted.

Enters room

This is a third grade class.

(To kids) Guys, this is an architect from London who came to meet us, how cool is that? David, his name is David. You know how to speak English.
KIDS Hello, Uncle! Hello David!
Hello!
RC   Over there, we have a glass window which gets a lot of the morning sun, and sometimes it gets very hot. So usually we use some shading when we can; sometimes it's just paper and it gets very hot, too hot. *(To kids)* Tchau gente! Bye bye!
KIDS Bye, Uncle!
Bye!
RC   Here it gets worse, right? We have a broken window, but with the current budget we can't fix it. We also have to install something here which is part of a project from City Hall, called *Educopedia*. It's like a portal they have created with activities—but we have to spend a great part of the budget to do this electrical installation.
This was my classroom last year, when I was still a teacher. Poor ventilation and dirt, which accumulates, gave us a serious problem and we had this water leak problem here. The leakage started at the residence, you know that there is a residence upstairs? Have you heard of it? There are children who live here, during the week.

Yes, we have heard about that programme. But it is still active in the CIEP schools?

RC   Not in all of the CIEPs. And there are children who no longer study here but they continue living here. That boy studies here, but this one does not; this one does, and he doesn't study here anymore.

And the kids, don't they have parents?

RC   Yes, they do. Most of them can go home on Saturday and Sunday, in theory, but some families don't come to pick them up. They have 'social parents'.

So this leakage problem, is it unique to this CIEP or is it the same in all of them? Do you think it has something to do with the way it was built?

RC   The slabs. It's because they are pre-fabricated slabs. In some of the schools the directors closed up all of the half-walls to the ceiling, with bricks. And these doors didn't exist. We had only shelves to put things.

Yes, I guess they would have been pre-moulded in concrete if they were part of the original design.

RC   Ah, that's true. I think it was done during the refurbishment. Originally this was not meant to be a classroom. It was maybe the science laboratory or a room for arts, because they have a sink. The white colour at this end is from the refurbishment; before it was all this dark colour. All the walls were this colour here, this grey.

Everything was grey?

RC   Yes. It made it a thousand times better, changing the colour. This building here is the first of the CIEPs, you know? This is the 001, right. It was built in 1984.

And there is one in Santa Cruz, that we also read about, where they did something different with the architecture…

RC   They are like that, very diverse. Because management bodies changed them as they went, as they thought necessary. Our building could never be changed that much, because it was the first one. We would be told 'No, we can't refurbish, no way.' And we could only do it when the Oscar Niemeyer Foundation came to do it…

I understand.

RC   Other directors started to raise the walls. When we received funds for the refurbishment project, that's what we thought was going to happen, that they would close them up to the top. Which was our dream, because those half-walls cause a lot of noise! It was unbearable at times; we could hardly teach. After midday, it was impossible, so in the afternoon I had to improvise and do different things because I simply could not speak anymore. My vocal chords became calloused. It's a serious issue, because it's a question of teachers' health really being impacted by the design.

And the students, are they from different background?

RC   Here we cater for the Santo Amaro and Tavares Bastos neighbourhoods, largely. But we also have a larger public who live in the suburbs, even kids from Baixada, Baixada Fluminense, who join their moms travelling to work very early in the morning. It's almost outside the city, in reality. To name some other neighbourhoods, they come from Caju, Bom Sucesso, Santa Cruz. Others come from São Gonçalo, where I live, near Niterói—they come with their moms. Their moms leave them here…

And the reason they come is because their parents work here, that's why they don't go to their local public schools, right?

RC   I think that it's also because we have this integral, full-day programme. It's not easy to find places that do the full day—more schemes are being implemented, but it was rare for a while. Here it's the same thing, the infamous half-wall, nothing new. This classroom looks so pretty, it deserves a picture.

This is a nice shelf. It's so tidy.

RC   Yes. For this, we really count on the collaboration from the teacher. If the teacher is not organised, it's impossible. But it is something that is up to the teachers themselves—I can't lie, because we don't give them resources to decorate their rooms. Sometimes, between buying paint for the fences or buying materials to decorate the rooms, unfortunately we have to choose the paint.

And do the parents or members of the wider community contribute in any way?

RC   No, nothing. They actually do come forward, but because they want to know what we're doing rather than to offer a contribution. They want to participate in the school, but as monitors—it's not about a mutual partnership. Here is another typical classroom. *(Addressing teacher)* Patricia, can you excuse us for a second. Guys, just a minute! This is David, he came from London to see the CIEP, how cool!

KID 1   Why?

RC   He came to see you guys here in the CIEP.

KID 1   Ah, it's true, because I'm so beautiful, right?

RC   He came all the way from London. Do you know how to speak English?

KIDS   No! What's your name? Hello teacher! Hello!

Hello!

KIDS   Hello!

KID 2   Does he speak French?

RC   Why French? Is London in France?

KID 2   No! Where is he from?

RC   From London, in England.

KID 3   What's your name?

My name is David, What's your name?

KID 3   My name is Romão.

Romão. Nice to meet you.

KID 3   Nice to meet you too! *(Laughter from kids)*

RC   Tchau! 'Brigada!

KIDS   Bye! Bye bye!

(Top) At Catete, some of the half walls are filled in using the official Niemeyer solution (Bottom) Interior view of the octagonal library

Leonardo Peixoto and Silvestre, respectively acting as teacher and social parent, are deeply and personally embedded in the life of the CIEP Presidente Tancredo Neves and its surrounding community. We met at lunchtime on Friday 30 March, 2012, in the school kitchen—where cooks and staff were busily preparing rice, black beans, scrambled eggs, potatoes, juice, bread and fresh slices of watermelon.

Leonardo began teaching at a CIEP in Rocinha, the largest favela in Brazil; at the time of our meeting, he had been working with the city for just three years. However, Silvestre is an old hand at Tancredo Neves, actually living on site as a social parent for the last twelve years despite having his own home. He began working for the school at the age of eighteen in 1986. Both Leonardo and Silvestre consider themselves to be civil servants.

Later at the rooftop residences—Tancredo Neves being one of the few CIEPs still to provide these—a party to celebrate Easter was in full swing. Over a few brigadeiros (Brazilian chocolates) and a glass of guaraná soda, we discussed the relationship between community and school.

A Conversation with Leonardo Peixoto and Silvestre
The Teacher and The Social Parent

LP Did Renata explain the half-walls, why the half-walls were designed? The intention was to educate through your own behaviour; to speak in such a way not to bother the next room, so it was also about educating or training your own voice and volume.

But it doesn't work in practice?

LP It doesn't work. Some things have changed: for example, the original project would say where the directorate's office should be, where room X or Y would be, it would give you the specific location for each room. But most of the CIEPs today don't follow that plan anymore. Some schools even split one room in two, to create new spaces.

We chat by the maintenance room, and continue while walking around taking pictures

LP The colour on these walls is not the original one. The upper part used to be darker and the lower part, I don't remember exactly, but it was lighter—maybe beige, but not white, because you can see how dirty it would become.
I've been with the city for three years; my first year was at a CIEP in Rocinha. At the one there, they still have the half-walls and the original colours of paint, if I'm not mistaken. Here the sports court structure is at the side; on the roof, you have the residences. In Rocinha, you don't have this area here, so the sports court is on top, on the third floor. And the reading room too. The original design was for a separate structure, like it is here. But in Rocinha, it is also on top, as part of the third floor.
There are CIEPs everywhere you look. The sheer number of CIEPs is immense.
They were a state government project, but then they went through a process of municipalisation, they became part of the municipal government. But some remain part of the state, and for example one became part of the state university in Caxias—it is all structured like a CIEP but it belongs to UERJ *(Universidade do Estado do Rio de Janeiro, Rio de Janeiro State University)*.

We wanted to see CIEPs in different contexts. This one is in the middle of a busy neighbourhood; Rocinha and Borel are different contexts again. But we wanted to see one in a rural location, more isolated…

LP There's one in Belford Roxo, in Baixada Fluminense. The one I am thinking about is on top of a hill in an urban area, but not the same kind of urban as here. You still have people crossing with horses, a big Sunday street market, so it's a more rustic-urban. *(Laughs)* From here to the Lake Region within the state of Rio, you see different settings; for example in Tanguá you can see one by the roadside.
And some of these are really interesting. If I'm not mistaken, with regards to the windows, they are all coloured in different ways: the school in Gávea links to the Regatas Flamengo football club, so the windows are red and black like their colours.

We continue to the outside area, by the playground

LP Over there is the original reading room. It is not square, it has more sides and that's the original design. I don't think I have the keys, but you can see it from the outside. The windows were glass originally. The room's construction is original, although we have refurbished the ceiling. And other CIEPs have this room too.

Is it not in use?

LP Yes, it is in use. We use it like a library, someone is responsible and the children can take books home. There are some things that I don't understand; for example, the sound issue. I think it's a great proposition with the half-walls, but it's very difficult. You need a really strong pedagogic programme, to educate both teachers and children. I also don't really understand these bars in the wall. To me, they compromise ventilation.

> **And the light too, right?**

LP   Actually, the light is not so much of a problem. When you have large windows, the glare of the sun does reach the blackboard at some point but with the bars it doesn't, so they protect it. But regarding ventilation, it is definitely a problem. Maybe because we no longer have the half-walls; maybe they would work together, as a combination of factors Now we have fans, but I don't know about the original project. Some CIEPs nowadays even have air-conditioning. The state had a project to acclimatise the CIEPs, so the ones that are state-owned got air-conditioning. Temperatures in the summertime can reach 48 degrees here, so it gets crazy. Although when it gets cold, the classrooms can get quite chilly.

We walk around, taking pictures

LP   They have been trying to bring back a curriculum that is not so much about culture, but rather based on knowledge.

> **And how about the cultural animators?**

LP   As I understand it, the municipal CIEPs no longer have them. But when I was at Rocinha, for example, there was a federal government project—I think called *Mais Educação (More Education)*—and they have some workshop leaders there.

> **So you didn't experience them?**

LP   No—this CIEP is as old as me! We are both from 1985. I have only experienced the CIEPs in the last few years and all of them were municipally-owned. None of them had the original animators anymore.

The kids come spilling out of class. We are now in the cafeteria.

> **Regarding the Mais Educação project, is that an attempt to reintroduce the full-time curriculum?**

LP   Actually, they identify schools that are ranking lower on student achievements and provide support for projects to get the children to do additional workshops—not taught by teachers but by new, local staff. So, as we are in Catete, we would get someone who is local, with local experience to run one of these workshop sessions.

Leonardo explains our visit to cafeteria team, Cristiana, Marta and Beth

Beth   The CIEP is beautiful, it's only a shame that Brizola died, you know.

LP   That's how everyone feels. Everyone here thinks that the CIEPs project was a beautiful idea which got lost. Some teachers here have been here since the beginning.

Beth   If only the governments that followed had cherished it. To think that students coming from poorer backgrounds and risk areas could even stay here…

LP   We installed these speakers to be able to play music for the children, for example during the lunch break. Something to calm them down!

> **What type of music?**

LP   We have played the Beatles! We sometimes play instrumental classical music, and samba or forró for children. On the opening day of this space, we played the Beatles.

> **Do you think this is something that other CIEPs have done?**

LP   No, installing the music system was our own initiative. We celebrated the reopening of the cafeteria. The school used to be rather messy, but then the director created a programme called *Quem Ama Cuida (Who loves it, Cares for it)*, starting by refurbishing the cafeteria. Some things were refurbished, but we couldn't complete the painting. The director was able to get towels and other decorations through donations, and there were flower arrangements on each table. These colourful things were not here before. The director was going to retire so we installed a little plaque with her name. We fitted some covers on the tables, to make it feel new. We added the music last year and now we have this.

The canteen at Tancredo Neves seats 200, and is situated between two small gardens that students are encouraged to explore and maintain

What are these numbers?

LP   They are the class numbers. That's where they line up in the morning. Some people are in favour of lining up others are against it...

And you?

LP   I'm against it. *(Laughs)* But it is still organised like this. In my class—in the second year—we held a debate the other day, after someone hit someone else while standing in the line. It was a debate about using violence and I asked the children if they thought it was right or not. The pupil who hit the other one suggested that there should be a jury. So that's what we did: we set up a jury with a 'lawyer' to defend each side. The lawyer defending the aggressor (person who hit the other) said that the real culprit was me, because I'm the one who made them form a line. If they hadn't been put in that position, then they would not have fought. Which is what I think, really! We try to create so many rules and structures, but it ends up generating more conflict. If things were a little less oppressive, it would be better. You can't leave everything loose, but it could be less oppressive. The lining-up, for example, is one problem that could be avoided. Sometimes a teacher spends a full ten minutes just trying to get them to form a queue. My class is really great, very interesting. We discuss all sorts of things, for example about sexual diversity. We talk about different themes around games between boys, games between girls, and in families. I am actually researching and finishing a Master's degree about this now.

We reach the auditorium

LP   I've been here for the past year but I have only used this space once. To tell you the truth, last year we stored the toys from the playground here, in lieu of nowhere else to put them. We do have a theatre teacher, but she only runs about four classes here. She rehearses plays, and when they are staged for outside audiences, they use this space. Now, I am thinking about using the auditorium or theatre as a cinema, too; I went to the cine-club, they will donate a video recorder, projector and a screen. In the future, we hope to have editing equipment too, so that children are not just learning by watching films but also by making them.

AA   Do you think this CIEP is in a better state than others? It's looking great; there are some leaking problems upstairs, but overall it seems really well maintained.

LP   Yes. *(Lowers voice)* If you go to the one in Rocinha, you will get a shock. No maintenance, you know. Here, we had a director that remained in her position for many years; she has only just left and she even donated some of her own money to this school.

Is the CIEP used for any external reason, beyond all the school functions?

LP   No, it is mainly used as the school. Sometimes it is used for hosting public exams, or as a polling station , or by *Viva Rio*, a social NGO based nearby. But the city needs to sign off on anything like that, so mainly it is used for public purposes.

We walk towards the sports court

LP   That area behind the court also belonged to the CIEP, but the City forced us to give it up to the Municipal Guard. We actually wanted to build a memorial here, a 'Centre for Memories', since this is the first CIEP.

Here we have the number of students that the CIEP can actually host, so we don't have so many problems. But in Rocinha for example, the CIEP is overloaded. If each room was designed for around 30 children, they would have 60. And then with the half-walls, it becomes a real problem.

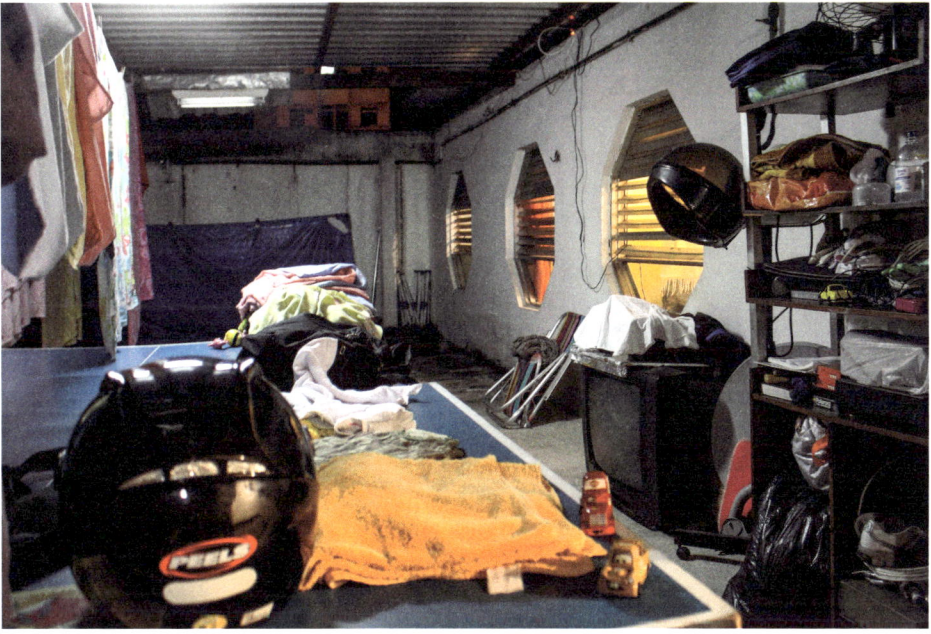

Penthouse suites: the living room (top) and private terrace (bottom) of the diminutive rooftop residences at CIEP Presidente Tancredo de Neves

KID Are you looking at the Christ? I live very close to it.

Some children come here from far away, don't they?

LP Yes, I have students from Belford Roxo whose mothers worked in Copacabana, so this CIEP would be on the way.

Is there criteria to select the students?

LP There are no restrictions. Only space. If there is space, we accept them.

We continue to take pictures and talk to the children. Leonardo leaves us inside the reading room, while the children help to turn the lights on.

LP The kids come here more often than the teachers.

Is it open during the day for them?

LP Yes, during their breaks they can come in here. But only when the reading room supervisor is here. We usually have three, because this room also serves other schools. But now we only have one, she comes five times a week; she opens it during the lunch break, during playtime and brings classes here for special activities. Some of the shelves are empty because they had old books that were no longer relevant, so we donated them. Now the supervisor is restocking the library with new books.

One difficulty we do have here—which is why we've put the window filters on—is that this room is very visible and so it is not safe. We don't leave computers here, for example. It's very tricky, the issue of security. Unfortunately, although we might dream of an ideal school open to all, we still need to have bars on windows—that's the reality. To have a computer here, we would need to build a locked space to store it. The TVs in the rooms, if you hadn't noticed, are surrounded by bars. It's not pretty and it's sad, but it can't be any other way. You have to watch TV through the bars. If you use the room in the evening, others outside can see everything in here.

Do you have any police security here?

LP No. Last year, we had a debate around security, whether to have police in schools or not. I am part of a group against it. What we got after that is door guards—people who register who comes in and out, which we didn't have before. We didn't even have an inspector for the large areas during the breaks.

Yes, because the open spaces are very large, so for teachers to have to monitor their classes plus everything else…

LP All classes use this space at least once a week, because it is mandatory to have one lesson in the reading room. But the students end up coming more than once. And they can take books home for the weekend and bring them back on Monday.

The teacher has organised all these books here in different categories, adding her own personal touch, as we don't have enough money for a dedicated librarian.

What change would you prioritise in the school if you could change it?

LP It's hard, but I think it might be the use of the outdoor playing space. For example, we have a ping-pong table that is not used for ping-pong. I think we could try to have more games or activities in the playground—even drawing on the floor, games like *amarelinha* (hopscotch)—and more ideas about how the children could use their free time, so they would not just be running around or looking for distractions by the water tank and so on. Actually, this comes from a discussion I had in my class, the children said, 'We want more toys'. So we made some signs and marched around the school, and we went to the director to make our demands!

Maybe this is the real thing, even more important than playground toys: we have a full-time curriculum, but it is not a truly integral school programme. Darcy's project was about an integral full-time school programme. Even if the child did not stay a full eight hours but rather only five hours in school, they still had an integral education—covering issues of life as a whole. We don't have here for example, a space where children can learn about personal hygiene—to take a shower, to brush their teeth—even though some of these children don't experience this at home. There's one mother here who thinks it's right to send her five-year old child to school to wash the clothes. I actually bought shampoo, soap and taught him how to take a shower, because he didn't know how to do it.

This is a unanimous feeling among the people who worked with the original concept. There was a lot it got right. We could be providing an integral education, not necessarily just in terms of time, but the City is not interested. The idea is always to make things more uniform. The seven-hour day schools, this is a municipal project; it doesn't quite work that way, that's not an integral full-time curriculum. But they have media support, they are advertising it and now, with the Olympics…

Now it is really interesting to watch how each successive government tries to leave its mark on the school system, with their own new set of structures. It's amazing. They want to leave their mark not only with a different pedagogic approach but also with a different architectural project. We have different structures of education, even in terms of their architectural expression. I think the CIEP has been a great motivator for this. It has brought this attention to the architecture of schools—of the building meeting the curriculum.

We continue taking pictures and chatting as we walk around

LP   And as for Niemeyer, we pray that he does not go too soon, because the day he goes, all this will go to hell. Even if we don't maintain all of its original structures, this was the first CIEP, so there's a greater pressure…

Apparently the team originally taking care of the CIEPs was very big; the education secretary marshalled a large team to monitor the teachers and so on. Teachers would have ongoing supervisor visits and hold debates. And so perhaps at that time, even the half-walls were not so much of a problem, because you had staff who were well-trained to work within them.

Part 2

Have you been to the residence, Leonardo? Renata was saying she's never been. And do you know the social parents?

LP   Yes, we all know them very well. They are part of the staff, but the social parents stay here. They might have their own house too; Silvestre does, I think. But they are always here, they live here, even at the weekends and so on. Most of the children come on Monday and leave on Friday.

Renata was saying that some of the children's parents don't come to pick them up…

LP   Yes, that happens, so then they stay all weekend. Just to mention a security issue—the CIEP in Rocinha doesn't have all this open space, only one large space at the front. But they only had this type of fence as protection; it was otherwise open to the community. In the end, they had to put bars all around the area, linked with the concrete pillars—for security reasons—so the children couldn't use that front area after all.

The bars don't even solve the security problem, because when the drug dealers want to use the space, they simply break the lock, use it, do it again the next day, and on Monday they would actually give us a new key! You see, back in the day, there was a patch of land where they would hold concerts at the weekend, and at those times part of the CIEP was the VIP Area. Down there would be the show, and the dealers would hang out here.

Then on Monday, someone would come on their behalf to give us a key for the new lock they had fitted, so that we could get in. As if nothing had happened.

And no one could say anything…

LP   I have a pupil who lives in Rocinha. Still now, under the UPP or 'pacification' measures, he says that the same stuff still happens; there is still a drug baron continuing his operations. Only this week, a community leader was killed inside Rocinha, so things like that are still happening.

The first pacified area in the suburbs was the Complexo do Alemão last year. And so one day I went to that region with a friend and we met some children from Vila da Penha, an area in Complexo do Alemão, and we had a chat about the Pacifying Unit. We asked them: 'So, is it better or worse now?'. They said it's a lot worse now with UPP. I asked them to explain—because you need to be able to ponder certain things, it's never black and white. They said: 'It's worse now, because with the dealers we had parties, we could walk around listening to music; now if we go around listening to loud music, they ask us to turn it off, they beat us…' So, it's not always like this with the violence, but you can see that it's also not quite like the media portrays it.

During the day, a different team works in the kitchen. In the original project, if I'm not mistaken, the food menu had to be diverse.

There was a nutritionist right?

LP   Yes, and there was breakfast, lunch and dinner. And lunch and dinner had to be different menus. There was a strong concern for nutrition. But now we use a syndicated network menu…

Here we are at the residences. In Rocinha, you would do this same journey to the top of the building, but in order to reach the sports court. This was the girls' residence, but it's closed as we don't have a female social parent—and no girls to shelter either.

Lots of children come to talk. We meet Vera, who runs the Student Residence programme for the school, and Silvestre, one of the social parents. Silvestre has been at the CIEP Tancredo Neves since 1986.

V   We have usually twelve children staying here, but now we have only nine. They live here for the working week, from Monday to Friday. Today there is a party for Easter.

Silvestre, as a social parent, do you live here permanently?

S   Well, I've lived here for just 12 years. But I first started working here when I was 18; my son was one month and four days old.

So your son lives here with you? Does he go to school here too?

S   Yes, he lives here with me, but he studies in Maria Leopoldina—a municipal college. He will be 27 in a month; I'm 45.

Who employs you?

S   It's the municipal government; I'm a public servant.

Do you know if other CIEPs have this role?

S   There used to be 45 social parents like me, but now there are only four.

And was the residency programme part of the CIEPs project from the beginning?

S   Yes. This CIEP first opened on 8 May 1985; I think the residency programme started only a month after that—and so it is, until today.

LP   But not all CIEPs have these residences.

Do you know which other CIEPs still have the residence?

S   There is one in Ilha do Governador and at Gávea *(CIEP Nação Rubro-Negra)* they have placed them on top of the reading room. One of my pupils from the residence is now in the army, studying his third year in military college.

What's the criteria to qualify for the residence—you don't have a lot of space, right?

S   Usually, the child has only one parent, either the mother or father, not both, so they are at risk. If the parent can leave the child here, they are then able to work. Now we only have nine spaces being used. But there is a selection process: they are interviewed, they go through a review system… The municipal government is in charge of it.

Do you have a waiting list?

S   Not at the moment, no.

Do you think it is strange that not all spaces are being used with so many social problems in Rio? I guess in many cases, the choice comes from the parents themselves to put their children here. So perhaps there are more children who need it, but whose parents don't want to take it up.

S   Yes, a lot of people don't know about the project or don't know enough about it.

V   It used to be well known, but slowly it started to fade out and end in many places. Not because of money problems, but rather due to the lack of social parents. The social parent does not have a financial incentive. He only receives his own salary. If he or she doesn't have the financial incentive, they go looking for something else. Because to take care of twelve children without an incentive…

Do you have to have any qualifications?

V   No, the only prerequisite is being a member of staff at the CIEP.

S   And to really enjoy doing it. Even though I don't get any additional benefits, I really enjoy the work.

Do the children have to pay?

V   No, nothing. So, now you can really 'embrace' the project. Please do promote it!

LP   We still have a problem to create a dialogue with the community and he helps with that. Silvestre is an example—even a figurehead—of keeping a dialogue with the community. He has a direct contact with the parents. Even if the parents don't have their children staying here in the programme, they know that Silvestre is a 'parent' in the school. So they talk to him. The problems that Silvestre brings us are the same as those that come directly from parents.

During the last elections for direction of the school, I have no doubt that one team won over the other because of Silvestre's support. His and Teresinha's, another member of the CIEP staff with close community links; she lives in the favela. That was the main differential between the two possible directions. That's another thing that I think is cool, that the direction is selected by the community. Not dictated by the government.

The children are singing an evangelical song, as we ascend to the rooftop.

And it is like that in all of them?

LP   No, just the municipally-run ones. The state-run ones, I am not sure. And in some of the municipal ones, the director is chosen by the mayor, so it varies.

Leonardo tells Silvestre about his value to the school and community—as he explained to us before

S   I was born up there in that community, in that favela, up on the hill. And I intend to go back there. My brothers, they all live up there.

LP   Do you have a house outside of the school?

S   Yes, my house is on the hill. I also have a little apartment in Pavuna but I prefer to be in the favela, on the hill. We all know each other, we have fun…

Does the community help you?

S   Oh yes. If I go to someone asking for help, I know that person will do it.

I was only asking because downstairs, with regards to the classrooms, Renata mentioned how some teachers go out of their way to make the rooms nicer, they buy things with their own money. And she didn't feel like the families would help on that front.

LP   It is tricky: for example, we can't ask them for support for educational materials. The city is obliged to provide all of that. But with my class, if I need some clay, something the city doesn't provide, or a paint of a better quality, then parents do help. We don't make a habit of asking because we know they don't have a lot of money anyway. But when we do ask for a good reason, they do help. And this dialogue works better as a direct relationship between teachers or staff, rather than an announcement from the director.

Then and Now: archival image of the rooftop residences (top) and the same facility today (bottom) at CIEP Presidente Tancredo Neves

Chapter 7
The CIEP Is The Channel

Detail of the main facade at CIEP Doutor Antoine Magarinos Torres Filho in Borel, showing Oscar Niemeyer's disctinctive lozenge-shaped windows

CIEP Doutor Antoine Magarinos Torres Filho is located in one of Rio's more common urban environments: the heart of the favela of Borel, in Rio's North Zone, the more impoverished and dangerous half of the city.

This is a second-generation CIEP school, built during the latter Brizola administration. It is an example of a compact CIEP, featuring a rooftop multipurpose hall and a double-storey library which host a residence for twelve children on its upper floor.

Bullet holes pockmark the walls, a result of the school's no-man's land location between two rival favelas—controlled by rival gangs—whose shoot-outs placed the building squarely in the crossfire. Long out of bounds, the recent reopening of the rooftop marks a small but significant success for recent pacification efforts.

The CIEP Torres Filho has since become integral to the work of the UPP (Unidade de Polícia Pacificadora, or Police Pacification Unit). The UPP Social initiative was set up after the pacification process began in 2008, onerously tasked with building trust, liaisons and dialogue between the favela community, its entrenched illegal economies and the newly established police presence. Here, at one of the only architect-designed buildings in the otherwise informal favela, we met the locally assigned officers.

The CIEP in Borel sits across the road from the popular Unidos da Tijuca samba school. Samba is an important, integral part of the local identity, and the current school director feels compelled to add percussion classes to the curriculum, despite the discontinued funding for the animation programme. Inside the bright blue octagonal library, we met samba teacher Francisco, a.k.a. 'Chiquinho'. Minutes before beginning a musical workshop, Chiquinho was setting up percussion instruments: caixas, tamborins, agogô bells, surdos, ganzás, cuícas, timbas and pandeiros. Their primal, pounding rhythms session resonated in the sultry air behind us, as we continued our tour through CIEP's well-tended garden.

An improvised wall construction modifies the covered arcade at ground level, at CIEP Doutor Antoine Magarinos Torres Filho in Borel

Lenita de Sousa Vilela is the principal and director of the CIEP Doutor Antoine Magarinos Torres Filho in Morro do Borel, located in Rio de Janeiro's impoverished North Zone. Banking over twenty years of experience at the same school, Lenita is a passionate principal who took immense pride in showing us around, explaining the improvements, adaptations and general condition of the school's physical environment—as well as pointing out the bullet-ridden walls, scars from the area's violent past. On the morning of Monday April 2nd, 2012, when we visited, we came across a traditional drummer setting up in the school's octagonal library block. The CIEP Torres Filho is situated across the road from the Unidos da Tijuca samba school, frequently animated by the sights and sounds of the fiercely competitive samba culture. Drawing from the CIEPs initial intention to provide the students with 'cultural animators', Lenita often invites professional musicians to give lessons at school. In this way, the CIEP reifies local and native culture as well as traditional academic subjects.

A Conversation with Lenita Vilela
The Director

LV   I have a few concerns when talking about the work of Mr Niemeyer. I admire him, but I am also critical of some things, okay?

That's not a problem, you can feel free!

LV   This building took nine years to complete, because it was being built on top of the only leisure space that the community had. There was some resistance from the community. During construction, there were serious problems because of the heavy rains: many houses were falling apart, the river flooded… The construction site actually housed many people following the floods of 1988.
At the beginning of 1992, the works resumed and were finally completed. But there was also an issue of security, unfortunately, before the 'pacification'. Twenty years ago, things were a lot worse: building materials would arrive, but they would be stolen, and the builders could never finish the work. Only when people from the community were hired as guards, construction workers and so on, then the building could be built…

So there was a lot of participation from the local community in the creation of the school? Has that continued into the present day?

LV   Yes, very much. Well, I have stories about this particular school; as for the others, I don't know. If you notice, it's a school without too much physical degradation, graffiti… That is because the community sees the school as something that is here to serve them, you understand? Of course, there are always one or two cases, hardly worth mentioning, when someone does something silly. But overall, the community helps take care of the school. Thank God that here you find an organised school; unfortunately not all the CIEPs are like this.

So how much has the school changed in the last two decades—both in its architecture and the programme? What about the half-wall classrooms, are they still here?

LV   They are still here, my darling. This one room is special: it is the only one that has been sealed with masonry because of the air conditioner and the equipment inside. In other schools, there is the same grid structure to keep goods safe, namely the computers. I would prefer it if it wasn't there, especially because—thank God—I haven't had any problems with people breaking in. But because it is a structural thing, it comes as a standard element—so it's the same all over. In the other half-wall classrooms, I have provisionally closed spaces off with screens, wooden screens. Although you will see that upstairs I have started to close it with proper partitions, which are more pleasing. There is a solution of louvres to more adequately close the classrooms, designed by Niemeyer himself. However, it's very expensive. It addresses acoustic issues and ventilation, but it's not viable within our current budget. For this reason, we chose the screens and partitions: they don't interfere with the structure and so they allow for the future possibility—when we have the money—for Niemeyer's designs to be used. Oscar Niemeyer, with Darcy Ribeiro, envisioned a different kind of school. This is the philosophy of the CIEPs: an open school, open to everyone, where the classroom does not belong to the teacher, but to everyone. But I think that they forgot that children have very high voices! With the half-wall construction, when one classroom is reading aloud or is singing, the other can't do anything. Here we are, hearing the noise from the dining hall downstairs. Now can you imagine half-walls besides half-walls? It's not possible. All teachers in the school—in fact all teachers in schools with this structure—developed throat problems.

On the other hand, the structure is very good for accessibility, for those people with disabilities; the ramps makes it easy for wheelchairs. Classrooms in other schools are not usually as big as the ones in the CIEPs. The structure is good, it's solid, strong, but I did have to rewire the electrics. And we also resurfaced the roof—not this one, but above the court. The sports court is all made in modules. Either it was not well done or it was old and tired, but if it rained, water leaked through the court into the floor below. So it was resurfaced really well and now I don't have any leaks.

But you will find other CIEPs in an appalling condition. Here you see a school in a good state, because it has had the same director for a long time; because my team and I, we take care of things; because the community helps maintain it—just as the school is a partner for the community, the community is a partner for the school.

We all do our bit to maintain the school. Not, unfortunately, as much as I would like to: there are challenges which you have to manage. For example as a public body, I can only give work to certain registered contractors and suppliers, so that the payment, insurance and everything is done properly in the appropriate time.

> **So it doesn't always need to be done via Niemeyer's foundation or offices? Unless you change the structure, right?**

LV   Exactly. Niemeyer's office only interferes if you are doing a significant modification. For example, I wanted to close the half-walls with bricks. My directorate sent this request to Niemeyer's office and it was denied. But as the problem of the walls was so widespread and there were so many requests, they had to permit a temporary solution.

> **Do you believe that each school should have a certain level of autonomy to develop—not only with regards to the architecture, the spaces through time, but also adapting to the local needs?**

LV   Yes. I think that every school director should have the autonomy to manage the space where they are working. But I do understand that an architectural work made by an artist—and Niemeyer is such an artist—should have some sort of protection, so that the work is not completely changed. I think that his office should have this ongoing project, to understand what's working and what's not working. I have never received a single questionnaire from anyone in his office, asking whether the half-wall worked or not. I have never been involved in any kind of survey, you know? Are you only looking at the physical structure or also the pedagogy, the fact that it runs a full-time schedule?

> **Yes, of course. And that's why it's really valuable to speak to you. Some people think that as architects, we are only interested in the physical aspect of the building. But we are really interested in the radical curriculum and the idea of the integral or full-time school. So to repeat the same question for the original curriculum, the vision: how has it changed over the years?**

LV   Well, in reality, what Oscar Niemeyer and Darcy Ribeiro envisioned for the CIEP has changed a lot over the years. They created the school to be an integral, that is to say full-time, school, with the staff performing a number of functions to allow for that to happen. But over the years, for a number of reasons, this personnel structure was really slashed. There was a reduction of staff because of financial difficulties, because the government has a fiscal responsibility in relation to the number of employees at City Hall. I started to work at the school with very few people; now, under Mayor Eduardo Paes' government there's been a slow increase in the number of assisting staff, so that we can start to look again at a full-time school schedule. There is a project called *Escolas do Amanhã (Schools of Tomorrow)* which identifies 150 schools in conflict areas, recently pacified areas or which will still be 'pacified'—although not all of these schools are CIEPs. In that programme, there is a project run by the Federal Government called *Mais Educaçao (More Education)*, which pays for workshops at the end of the school day, when the children would normally be leaving. But the CIEPs is already a full-time school programme, we already run an afternoon shift. I have judo workshops, graffiti workshops, capoeira—additional opportunities which allow a child to stay the whole day in school. And so they can enjoy it, rather than school feeling like a prison. Because here, it is sometimes necessary for a child to spend nine hours in school each day.

>**What exactly are the daily hours here?**

LV   The children arrive in the early morning, they have breakfast here, then go off to the classroom; they study, have lunch here, then back to the classroom. The little ones even have a nap in the classrooms, then they wake up and there is a diverse series of activities in the afternoon—art or music activities, or physical education. Finally they have dinner and then they leave. I have one group of students which leaves at 2:45pm, but that's a small group – the majority leave at 6:30pm.

>**There was this original idea that the curriculum was tailored to the local culture. Does this happen here—and would you have any examples?**

LV   Well, to speak of a really local culture... I think it's actually regional culture. I think this is a concern even from the Secretary of Education, to make things work in the best way possible. What do I have here? I have people from the local area who come to do some of the workshops, in graffiti, capoeira, street art—people from the community who come to work with the children as part of this 'More Education' project.

>**That's what I was going to ask. We saw a school that offered judo or something like that as an extra curricular activity, but the local community was more familiar with capoeira, you know? Was there a pressure to offer activities that fit a more local culture?**

LV   For example, our school is in front of the *Unidos da Tijuca* samba school. So because this music is in the blood of these children, I chose to include a percussion workshop. They have a percussion class, because all children love samba and they love music, the drums, the beat. This is one kind of regionalism.

>**Do you think that a uniform building, with the same architecture and the same curriculum—because they are the same in all CIEP schools—can suit different locations? Do you think that it works regardless?**

LV   Yes. Because we all belong to the same network, the City Hall. The jurisdiction of City Hall runs from the West Zone—which is Campo Grande, Santa Cruz—to Paquetá, which is that island; so all the children do the same exams. In these matters, there's no discrepancy. What is different, then? One workshop or another, which has a touch of the community, the presence of specific community members: that's what I think the adjustments are. In relation to the standard curriculum—that's what makes Brazil speak the same language from North to South. We have this characteristic. We like everything mixed together, but with a guiding axis, you know? We have many accents but the same language, right? I think it's a Brazilian characteristic—that's the way I see it.

>**That's interesting. The architecture is concrete, it's quite brutal. What's it like to maintain, what are the difficulties?**

LV   The school is very big. It is easy to maintain, but the difficulty is in maintaining such a big building. The size, I think, is the most difficult part. But you also have a structure, which is pre-moulded, there's no way to escape it, you know? I have made a few adaptations: I've adapted the bathrooms—you will see the bathroom I did work on and the one I didn't. The bathroom which I haven't done any work on yet is very ugly. The flooring is different, really...

> **I don't know if you have them here, but in Catete they still have the student residences, from the 'Social Parent' programme…**

LV   No, we don't run that here, because the residence where the children would live faces the favela. This school was often in the line of fire from stray bullets, during the violent periods in Rio. And the Social Parents programme is really a declining project; it's not moving ahead, so they don't really discuss it anymore.

> **Do you have an opinion about the project?**

LV   I think that a child's place should be with the family, not only at school.

> **Well, two more questions. One is regarding the cultural animation programme. I know that you mentioned various workshops…**

LV   We don't have the cultural animators anymore. Actually, this school has never had a cultural animator. The only entertainer is me! Ha ha ha…

> **The last question: can you imagine a new generation of CIEPs being built in the future? If so, what would you change about the project?**

LV   I would keep the integral, full-time schedule, but I would add more staff. Because really, the school is so big, you need a lot of supporting staff. I really think that is what's lacking, it's really tiring. You have to run up and down after the children, and we get tired. I would keep the integral structure, and the size of the school is very good. Today, I actually host a school within the school. There used to be a kindergarten in the next street, but the building was falling apart. So we are now temporarily hosting a daycare centre in what used to be our auditorium, with three little classes which cater for 60 children, toddlers aged between two and three.

Part 2

LV   Here is a better version of the temporary wall partitions, let's say.

> **That's a more permanent one.**

LV   This is my office, where I work. I mean really, I can't even put in an air-conditioner —during the 40-degree heat we have all summer. That's a big problem.

> **Do you know what the objective was in having the half-wall even in your office? Was it the same reason?**

LV   The entire school is built with half-walls, my darling. The school is for everyone. There is not one single room, you see? It's a massive socialising space. Let's go…

> **Ah, the auditorium was here?**

LV   The auditorium was here. We've got some funding to paint this first floor, but the second one is not painted. Let me show you the modified bathroom, where we changed the floor. But the bathrooms will probably be dirty, ok? Here we adapted the space for small children, from the kindergarten…

> **But there were already showers before, right?**

LV   Yes, but those are upstairs. These days, only the little ones take a shower here. These are all adaptations, the bathroom was not like this. But please use Photoshop to get rid of the dirt! Or you could wait—you see, we clean it when the children are sleeping. This small toilet seat for the infants, we did that too.

> **Ah, we also saw this sort of thing in Catete too.**

LV   Yes. I'll show you the way we have been closing up the rooms upstairs. We are installing internet connections, computers and display equipment in each room, but we are starting upstairs, with the older kids. Over there we adapted the balcony ledge so that children don't spit or throw little things from up here, as they sometimes do… Although my main worry was that they would lean over it.

But did you need permission to put these things here?

LV No, because they're made of wood. *(Walking on)* Memories from the past: that is a bullet mark. There are more. And we would lie on the ground to hide, crawling on the floor. Until the saviours of the nation, until my heroes would arrive!
Over there is the *Unidos da Tijuca* samba school. And there is the reading room, the library; above us would have been the social parents' residence. Now a staff member lives there, he works as a caretaker. And here is the access to the sports court. Don't just take pictures of the ugliness, ok? It has a good functional structure...

And you put paper here on the windows, because of the sun?

LV Yes, for the light and also because the activity outside can be distracting for the children, right? It could have been curtains but the teacher thought that paper would allow for a better use space, as another visual resource.

Do you think, then, that you would like to install air conditioners in more places?

LV I'd like to. My goal is to have air-conditioning in every classroom. Because it's maddening, the heat. You notice that each room has three fans and they still don't work... We took the wooden partitions here out; later we will complete the paintwork as it is on the second floor.

Did this adaptation need permission?

LV No, not this one either. Because it is removable, it can be placed and re-placed and it does not affect the concrete structure.

Who sets the regulations? Is it City Hall, or the Oscar Niemeyer Foundation - who decides what you can and cannot do to the building?

LV It's the city. City Hall, with the authorisation of the Foundation.

And what do they think of your modifications?

LV I don't think they even know.

I guess they don't have to know, because you are not affecting the structure, right?

LV I am not changing the structure; I have adapted within the structure.

Did you decide to adapt the building this way specifically so that you would not have to go through that bureaucratic process?

LV Exactly right. All the rooms will have internet, that's why we are putting the projectors in them... Over there is cabling for light, to turn the projector on, to turn the computer on. The internet will work wirelessly, with a router.

Doesn't all this heavy concrete affect the wi-fi signal?

LV Ah, that I don't know. The problem is that it's too hard for you to do anything. That's why I opted to fix the fans to the partitions, because the concrete is impossible to penetrate. Do you want to see the sports court?

Yeah, absolutely. It's so interesting.

LV Just before we go there, this should give you an idea of the classroom environment. How can you read here, with others talking over there at the same time? It's unfeasible. But can you see the access for wheelchair users? That's very good...

Arriving at the Multipurpose Room and outside area

So cool, the garden! So the kids work there and learn how to grow things? It's looking so pretty. Very tidy!

LV They are so respectful—thank God—people respect it. It's nice because the trees are big, but do you see that sink? There you clean the dishes and the dirt goes straight into the river. It is lovely, but it is a desperate solution. When we have a big event, we can hold it here in the Sports Court, while smaller gatherings can happen in the classrooms.

Now I'm in a bidding phase to change the security net here. But generally, this school is in good shape. If you visit the CIEP in Praça Sáenz Peña, oh my God.

We're going to visit the one in Rocinha, we hear it is a bit rough…

LV   The CIEP in the square? My dears, don't go. It is very run down.

Well, the objective of this project is to learn what worked and what didn't work in the CIEPs—it's about lessons learned.

LV   You could never have done this research before the pacification process, for a start. Someone would immediately say 'Why are you taking pictures? Why are you photographing us?' The local community had a unbelievable persecution complex. And everything was about them. I couldn't even say 'Do you see that house over there?' because they would say, 'Miss, why are you pointing over there?' That kind of thing.

I can imagine. And the change came very quickly? The UPP programme started in 2010, right?

LV   I loved the UPP, I was a poster girl. I was in advertisements with the governor, Sérgio Cabral. Perhaps I expressed my support a bit too much, I don't know if I'd do that now, but I wanted to give credibility to the UPP: that it was here to stay and that it was better for everybody. I wanted to give my testimony of what was happening, which was true. Because that was about public policy, not party policy—not just a policy of one government. It's a transformational policy and we, good citizens, are the ones who are going to make it work. We will scream and shout to stop the idea that violence would dominate our lives again. To say that now there will be order, there will be law.

Of course.

LV   One criticism: when you have to change a light bulb, you need to rig up some scaffolding to do it! And here is proof of how it leaked. Whenever it used to rain upstairs, it would go all the way through here.

Just so you have an idea of how it is used, we do graduations and other ceremonies on the roof of the court; for example, there was a convocation ceremony for a course run by the Military Police, here in the school. This wall was an early modification. Because I used to find inappropriate things here, like used condoms or other rubbish… Downstairs there used to be the CIEPs health centre. But I did not have professional staff, so the Health Secretary came to an agreement with the Education Secretary and we gave the space over to be used as a formal health centre for the wider community, run under the *'Programa Saúde da Família' (Family Health Programme)*. So it used to be a part of the CIEPs complex, but now it is used by the Health Department.

We are rethinking some of the playground features too. We received some playground equipment as a donation—but it is made entirely of plastic, so it cannot stay exposed to the sun. So we are going to shift the playground so it can be covered. And we are going to add a fence, so that the older children don't play in there. Over here will be a dedicated area for the older children.

And do you need permission to do this?

LV   No.

Ha! It is amazing how you find your own way of doing things. You have to adapt in different ways, because there's a lot of bureaucracy.

LV   You see, you can't do it. But it's an under-utilised space right now, just for children to run around during recess. We want to use the space more…

And to allow for some protection against the sun…

LV   Exactly. Now I'm going to show you the original bathroom and the dining hall. This bathroom is the only one I still have in its original form, which was quite ugly. Please don't show these images to Niemeyer's team, by the way! I'll know who the snitch is!

> I think it's really resourceful. The yellow colour scheme… Is that the original colour?

LV The bathroom is in the original colour. Back in the day, the chairs in the dining hall were yellow too, with the 'Full Time School' logo—a pencil like this, similar to the CIEPs logo. We still have one here.

> We do have the CIEPs book, with the little logo—it's like a piece of the Brazilian flag.

LV Yes, in the shape of a pencil. If you notice, it is a pencil.

> I see, we had wondered about that!

Walking on past the graffiti workshops

LV Nowadays when the weather is cooler, it's really quite cold here. Because it is so open, really, you can't cover it.

> It's like your house, isn't it? You feel, you know, proud of it? You seem to take care of it as if it was your own house.

LV Yes. Ha ha ha!

Page 162: The canteen at the Borel CIEP features handpainted murals; to celebrate its refurbishment, the school PA system played music by the Beatles
Overleaf: A class of students make the short walk from the main building to the library building. The library is designed to receive students as well as the outside community. Above, there is a student residence that can accommodate up to 12 children, under the care of a pair of adult social residents.

The social residents are public employees assigned to the CIEPs from the local community. The first sixty CIEPs received soldiers from the Military Police and the fire services. They are expected to define domestic routines and making sure that they attend classes. During the daytime social parents may undertake tasks like coordinating the canteen or cleaning and helping out in classes, or attending to problems with the school building itself.

Carlos Eduardo is a young police officer engaged with the CIEP Doutor Antoine Magarinos Torres Filho in Tijuca and its surrounding community. As he high-fived passing students on our visit, Carlos explained how the school has become integral to the work of the UPP Social (the social programme of the UPP or Pacification Police Unit).

Set up after the pacification process, UPP Social is tasked with building up trust, establishing links and maintaining a dialogue between favela community and the newly established police presence. Before the establishment of the UPP Borel in 2009, children and teachers became habituated to dropping to the classroom floor, in order to avoid getting caught up in daily exchanges of gunfire.

Just three years later, we saw children playing happily outside. The CIEP is one of the only architect-designed buildings in the otherwise informal favela; the rooftop sports hall hosts UPP workshops, debates and open forums, where the opinions and ideas from members of the community are heard and shared.

A Conversation with Carlos Eduardo
      The Policeman

> **How much do you know about the original CIEPs project? What do you think about the school?**

CE   I know that Oscar Niemeyer planned the physical buildings, but with regards to how the CIEPs would work, the idea was created by Brizola, who structured the project itself. The CIEPs were intended to give the child greater support; it is not an ordinary school. Here the children are fed and they have access to activities beyond the traditional school activities. That was the CIEPs' purpose: Oscar Niemeyer planned the physical structure, but that was the greater plan for the school.

And there's the idea of full-time school… They can stay in school for the whole day, rather than having to go home in the afternoon. The school provides opportunities for a number of activities, beyond the traditional curriculum; it teaches them about citizenship and discipline.

They have music classes, sports, other lessons that are really interesting for the development of the child. I studied a bit of pedagogy so I am biased, but I think the project is really interesting. Some of the CIEPs don't quite follow the original idea, but most of them do a really great job.

> **Would you prefer the original concept to be maintained—do you think it has changed much?**

CE   It has been changed, adapted, but for the better. This year, for example, the integral or full-time schedule is to be expanded. Most of the changes have been for the better and it is still about providing assistance to the children.

> **And what about the links between the CIEPs and the local community?**

CE   Most of the children here—in fact almost all of them—live in or near to Borel. So when we need to address the community, the school is that channel, connecting us with the children and also with their parents. It's an important channel, in our case: linking the police and the community, via the CIEP. And it is located right in the middle of the community, inside Borel.

> **How important was the CIEP in supporting the pacifying programme?**

CE   The CIEP opened the doors to dialogue, between the police and the community. Whenever there is need for an event, the director Lenita is very supportive, providing the space. Actually, when we had our one-year anniversary of setting up the Borel UPP station, the celebration was at the CIEP. We had a week of events, debating different themes in the neutral space of the school; the community joined in. We even had lectures in the evening to cater for people who work during the day. And when there is a CIEP event, we come along too. We are all really well known here; the children know us, and the teachers. They can call us, ask for help and there's a good level of mutual respect. Lenita was really instrumental in creating this link.

The police run an anti-drugs campaign called PROERD *(Programa Educacional de Resistência às Drogas e à Violência,* Drugs and Violence Resistance Education Programme*)*. All municipal and state schools usually have a police officer who comes to talk about drug resistance, up to fifth grade. It is part of the curriculum. In the areas with UPP, they have an extra demonstration for how the UPP works. We all take part, we do a workshop with the children, to show the day-to-day reality of the police—drawings to explain how the relationship used to be and how it is now, for example. Whenever there is a visit to museums, for example, the children come with us too; I think every child in the CIEP now has done a school visit with us.

So there are links through PROERD and we are also hoping to run more debates, as other UPPs are doing, to improve relationships with the children, their families and the wider community.

I think the CIEPs project will continue moving forward; although the physical structure and the original programme are getting old, there are improvements being made to both, and so it maintains its relevance. Education is a fundamental thing; our children are the future of this place—especially in places that have suffered from violence and urban warfare. The original project set that context and there is enough in there to make the CIEP a good and worthwhile project.

> What about the physical positioning of the CIEPs, in prominent spaces within the community—what impact does that have?

CE   Not only here, but in other areas with CIEPs, the positioning of the schools allows for most people in the community to walk between the CIEP and their homes, to pass by it often, to become physically familiar with it. Since the UPP post was established here, it's safe enough for many of the children to walk home because it's safer, whereas before they had to wait to get picked up. So the visibility and the easy access helps a lot. Although when it was built, there were not as many houses around here—the population in this neighbourhood has pretty much doubled in the last dozen years—but perhaps the school already anticipated that expansion.

> Do the parents get involved?

CE   I think the proximity actually helps with that; they do get involved. You always see them engaging in different activities and chatting to each other when they come to pick their children up… And some CIEPs have something called *Projeto Amigos da Escola, or Friends of the School*, an organised group of parents and members of the community who offer to give lessons on varied activities.

> Which of the CIEPs distinctive spaces are most used by the community?

CE   I think the computer room, the library and the sports court on the roof are the most used spaces. And sometimes some of the classrooms. There is also an annexe, just outside the school building, and that operates as a health centre.

> Could you image a new generation of CIEPs being built? What would you change or keep from the original?

CE   The physical structure is fine, but I would add even more projects for the children to go on visits outside of school, to have more leisure activities, links with museums and so on. I would expand the educational programme, not necessarily the physical building. I think it's great that we always see the children in movement, learning, in classes, using the outside spaces and so on. The CIEP provides a programme which means that the children are always busy doing something.

The multipurpose room on the rooftop at CIEP Doutor Antoine Magarinos Torres Filho, a compact-designed CIEP (top and bottom)

Chapter 8
This Idea, It's Magic

CIEP Doutor Bento Rubião is another example of a compact design; Rocinha's dense, informal environment could only offer a small site

The CIEPs project is a powerful demonstration of an architecture, at once iconic and pragmatic, that is specifically made to amplify the importance of education. They are not perfect; certain flaws in Niemeyer's original design have required repeated attention over the last decades. For example, classroom conditions—like acoustic and thermal comfort—proved to be ill-considered for Rio's tropical climate. Clearly political in their symbolism, their failure was not due to the educational programme. Distinct and easily identifiable as the legacy of notoriously Socialist governor Leonel Brizola, the CIEPs fell victim to prejudice from the right wing electorate. In retrospect, it was perhaps ill-advised for a large infrastructural project to be expressed as such a radical political statement, therefore linked to a particular personality or ideology. The CIEPs success would be seen as a validation for Brizola's socialist ideals. Successive governments with markedly different political priorities felt obliged to distance themselves from the project, often withdrawing funding, maintenance and support. Luckily, the buildings have proved to be highly durable,

even with little caretaking. Today, the CIEPs are being painted, the grass is being cut and the current Secretariat of Education seems not to subscribe to the same stance as its political predecessors. Looking ahead, it seems that the state of Rio will need all of their CIEPs in the next 30 years, and possibly even more new buildings.

The CIEPs educational programme may have been arrested for political reasons, but the ideals are far from dead. At the time of writing, full-time education was once again on the agenda in Brazil, as highly strategic for the future success of the country. Signs point towards the continued intention to provide and integrate high-quality schooling in otherwise underprivileged neighbourhoods, and to continue to welcome the wider community into the school.

An allotment in the playground of CIEP Doutor Antoine Magarinos Torres Filho in the Borel neighbourhood

Claudia Costin is the Senior Director for Education at the World Bank Group. Before joining the World Bank and at the time of researching this book, Costin was Secretary of Education for the Municipality of Rio de Janeiro (2009–2014). Under her stewardship, learning results across the city rose by a fifth. With a strong belief in the transformational power of education, Costin also helped to create Todos Pela Educação (Education for All), a civil society movement founded in 2006.

Holding a PhD in International Education and Development from New York University, Rafael Parente is the director and founder of LABi (Laboratório de Inovação Educacional or Laboratory for Educational Innovation) and the educational start-up Aondê. He was the undersecretary of New Educational Technologies for the Municipality of Rio de Janeiro from 2009 to 2013.

On Wednesday April 4, 2012, at Rio de Janeiro's imposing City Hall, a conversation with Claudia and Rafael allowed us to reflect on the CIEPs' reception over the past decades, before mapping potential future directions for public education in the city.

A Conversation with Claudia Costin and Rafael Parente
   The Politicians

   How do you think the CIEPs method of teaching has changed, how different was it from what is being provided now?
CC   In the beginning, with Darcy Ribeiro, the CIEPs offered regular classes in the morning and then in the afternoons there were after-school programmes: arts, sports, some school support. Later, people appointed regular school teachers to run the afternoon programme, but that didn't work very well. The teachers don't have the right training for after-school activities in the arts and so on.
So, after discussing how to adapt the original proposition, we decided simply to have more hours of classes, just as you do in Great Britain or in the rest of Europe—a seven-hour curriculum, with after-school activities on top of that. But those are not with teachers, they are run by paid professionals who can teach dance, drama classes, run science clubs and things like that. So that is the evolution where we stand now. Not in all of the CIEPs, but in many of them.
RP   The ambition is to reintroduce the full-time curriculum in all the CIEPs, right?
CC   Yes, to all of them. You know, the best school—because we are having external assessments now—the best school in Rio in 2010 and in 2011 was a CIEP. And now the CIEPs are competing: which is the best *school*, not the best CIEP. One of the CIEPs in a violent area—*CIEP 1º de Maio* in Santa Cruz—was named 'Best School' in 2010.
   Is the new full-time schedule going to be compulsory or voluntary?
CC   It's voluntary. Well, the seven hours a day is mandatory, and this is a major change. And the two extra hours of after-school classes are really there if it's useful for parents, or if the kids want it. That way, you have a little bit more of the original idea of an open school: a school that opens itself to the community. When it was decided that only teachers would work in the CIEPs, it did systematise things in a way—but on the other hand, we lost some of the idea that the CIEP is not only a school, it's a cultural centre for the community. It's open for the community, so teaching and learning spreads through the neighbourhood; the neighbourhood is welcome in the school.
   How is that going to be achieved, going forward?
CC   Well, it's happening already. This after-school programme, involving local community members with their own skills, their own talents, that is happening since August 2009 with the support of the Ministry of Education. It's called *Mais Educação (More Education)*. It's amazing what's going on. It depends a lot on the quality of the School Principal, you know, like everything else. It's not that you can be 100% certain that programmes work superbly. But when you have a wonderful Principal, Mais Educação is amazing.
For example, in Maré, there are lots of talented people related to dance, and so you can have the best talent going in to teach our kids. The kids are exposed to local expertise, and they can imagine their lives differently—because Maré, for example, is an area controlled by the narco gangs. And so if they can see talented people that aren't connected to the narco-trafficking, they can imagine their lives differently. In Cidade de Deus, another area that has been very recently pacified—pacified means that the narco-trafficker guys were…
   They were removed?
CC   Repatriated, yes. The urban territory was returned to Brazil. Well, in Cidade de Deus, there is somebody teaching the kids how to fix bicycles after school. He's not a teacher, he is the owner of a small bicycle repair shop.

So do you think that this after-school element relates to the original idea of cultural animation?

CC   Yes, I do. It works much better than using only teachers for these activities; they are already exposed to teachers seven hours a day, and teachers have their own way of teaching. Being exposed to different kinds of people, who complement their work—this means that their repertoire widens.

RP   I would add that it's a more hands-on practice, rather than being too didactic, too much talking, you know. Teachers like to talk a lot in front of the kids, but people in the communities are more hands-on, teaching by doing.

CC   Also something interesting happens: sometimes kids get the impression about their regular instructors that 'Yes, they are teachers and that's what teachers are supposed to do, how teachers behave'—and that back in real life, things are different. If they see adults from their own neighbourhood, their own background, others who have different talents, and who are not teachers... For example, it's a very feminine world, the world of schools. So if they see some guys with different skills, or if they see some women who are now professional, you know, it's also good for the kids.

RP   They can even work as role models for them, showing them different possibilities.

CC   Yeah, role models. That's definitely it.

What about the original idea of the social parent, where some children who would be living within the CIEPs schools, on the other levels—does that still exist?

CC   It has diminished a lot. We do still have people living in the schools, *'o residente'*, but not that many. Nowadays the preferred thinking is to link those kids within their family structure. It's not that we didn't want to keep the residential programme going, but now judges are strongly against that kind of approach. So we only have kids living in the school when there's absolute certainty that they cannot be raised in a family home.

Do you personally think the residential programme was a good idea?

CC   I think the judges exaggerate a little bit. Because for some parents it's convenient and the family link is so broken; you cannot insist on something that you know for certain is not working. For example, we have parents who are drug users, addicted to crack. How can you rebuild a relationship with a parent who is addicted to crack? Maybe once that parent has been treated properly – but that's unfortunately not the approach in most cases. So we don't have a lot of kids living in schools anymore, although it could be beneficial to boost this in the future.

Looking back at the CIEPs in their original form, what do you think is the most important aspect of the project—the architecture or the curriculum? Can you have one without the other, or do you think they are stronger when they go hand in hand?

CC   I think the curriculum is the most important. The architecture is important, the buildings help, but they don't teach. And there were a few decisions or experiments made in the buildings at the time, which in the end didn't prove to be so interesting. I'll give you an example. Darcy Ribeiro did not like the idea of enclosed individual rooms, with full height walls. But the half-wall system doesn't work for the normal teacher; Niemeyer had to change the design later, because all the teachers began to have problems with their vocal chords. There is just one CIEP school where I have heard of it working but they had a wonderful Principal who insisted on special training for his staff. It is not replicable, that's a one-off case. Ribeiro may have anticipated that everybody was going to talk quietly, but real teachers are not angels, they are normal human beings. Not to mention the students!

Then, there is the idea of the possibility for community life inside the school. I like this attitude, and I was very sad when I saw the way that some of the CIEPs were becoming ruined—nobody was cutting the grass, they were not painted, they were not maintained. This was because the later political administrations did not believe in the project—more so since the CIEPs had become a trademark of one politician, namely Leonel Brizola. Everybody wanted to disassociate from Brizola, and so there was an aversion to the buildings themselves. They began to be neglected. It was symbolic.

RP I think historically, there was a sense in the educational network here in Rio that the CIEPs were there to deal with the worst students. And not only the worst students but also the worst teachers, like a social prejudice. As you only came to teach at the CIEPs if you couldn't get a job somewhere else.

CC There was definitely a stigma. There was, and perhaps there still is some prejudice. When the *CIEP 1º de Maio* came out on top of the external evaluations as the best school, it was so embedded, this social prejudice, that people were claiming that the school had 'cheated'. It's an external evaluation! Cheating would be impossible!

> **Do you think there might be a new type of CIEP building programme in the future?**

CC I think the CIEPs project is part of our architectonic history. Now there are new materials for building; we are not bound to repeat the past forever. So I don't think that we will build more CIEPs exactly; there will be new ideas for new types of schools. There are advantages to the CIEPs approach. Sometimes if you have standardised schools, it looks too much… I'm not an architect, so I don't know the proper vocabulary. For example, in São Paulo they built the CEUs, a similar type of school building. It's another interesting school programme that came after the CIEPs; the CEUs also use the same building model everywhere. But sometimes you get the feeling that a CEU spaceship has just landed in the favela. They are interesting to look at, but could adjust a little bit more to the external landscape.

But I can also understand why you might have to standardise a little bit. In a poor country—well, we are not poor anymore, but we have poor areas—there is not a lot of money invested in education. And in my opinion, the bulk of that money should be spent on teaching and learning, rather than new buildings. So the inventiveness of architects might have to be constrained a little bit if you want to build on such a scale, especially as we now know that schools should be a little bit smaller to work properly. One of the CIEPs even had 3000 kids – but it doesn't work.

> **Do you think the space of the standard CIEPs campus is too big to control?**

CC Sometimes, yes. We've had problems with some CIEPs, because it's very difficult to supervise the grounds—some places are violent and sometimes gangsters take the opportunity to just go into the schools to rob the computers. But we found an interesting solution for that; we decided in those areas to insert a nursery school into the open space, and add an extra door. Effectively, you lessen the open space.

> **I recently heard that some of the CIEPs are now vacant or abandoned, that they are no longer functioning as schools. Is that correct?**

CC Not in the city. Perhaps some in the state. There's one that has been transformed into a fire department, which I think might even be illegal!

> **Could you see in the future some CIEPs being converted into other uses, because there are so many…**

CC If the population changes—I can't predict if we will definitely need all the schools forever. But I think for the next thirty years at least, we will need the CIEPs, certainly.

Plus, if we want to make all the schools run for seven hours a day—and I think that we should—then I expect that we will need more schools, not less, even if there is a demographic transition.

We heard about a CIEP installed in a former hotel, in Ipanema.

CC   You must mean the CIEP at Cantagalo. Oh, it's not very easy, that one—the *CIEP Presidente João Goulart*. First, the building was not originally designed as a school, and so it's very difficult to manage. It's beautiful, it has a swimming pool, and an NGO that runs that pool and some of the spaces. Can you imagine a CIEP with a swimming pool? But it's actually one of our worst performing schools. We are still in the process of discovering what went wrong there. It might be that the way the building was structured was not good for learning.

So you can't imagine the City of Rio embarking on a programme of reusing existing buildings?

CC   Sometimes it might work. For example, for small kids at nursery school level, sometimes we have used private houses, which can be transformed. But if you're looking at the model of the CIEP for today, I would suggest some changes. Firstly, close up the walls and use a better system of ventilation. Secondly, the water leaks—this is a problem with all of them. And more light, natural light inside. Niemeyer is wonderful with design but not with light.

Are you trying to reclaim the whole idea of the CIEPs, or re-plan the existing ones?

CC   We are not like Europe, which has a long history of architectural evolution. We have some buildings here that date from the beginning of the 20th century. But you don't throw away your history and the CIEPs are part of the history of education. So should we throw away these buildings? No. We have to renovate them and try to discover ways to take care of them properly. Perhaps in the future we will discover that another kind of building is more useful for teaching. But the CIEPs are part of this history, part of an important moment in the history of Rio, when there was this heavy investment in education. It was a time when they thought poor kids should have a better chance. You don't kill the programme just because some people believe that Brizola was a populist. We made an evolution of the initial CIEPs idea, in terms of prioritising tougher areas. In a sense, it's an evolution but also like 'Back to the Future'! We noticed that some schools are in areas controlled by the drug traffickers, or violent militias, or in areas that were very recently pacified. Those schools need extra help. Firstly, teachers don't want to teach there; it's not attractive to work in Maré, for example, because you know that conflicts might emerge, you might be exposed to risk. You will be in charge of small kids who are at risk too, and you will be the only adult present. So we decided to increase pay for the teachers working in the 151 underprivileged schools which have been selected as the *Escolas do Amanhã, or Schools of Tomorrow*. We also have a kind of a prize for teachers if kids improve their learning. It's not exactly a bonus, but it's a prize.

Like a target?

CC   We don't compare schools. But if the performance of the kids makes a big improvement in an external evaluation, then all the teachers, the cook, the cleaners, everybody in the school receives an extra bonus that year. If that school is a 'School of Tomorrow', instead of just receiving one bonus, they will receive one and a half, because it's harder to teach in violent areas. In addition, we changed the way we teach science in the schools; we built science labs inside each classroom, so they learn science by experimenting—and they love it, kids love the way we teach science. And they have this after-school programme, the *Mais Educação* in all of them. What else?

RP   We have brought back the *Saúde nas Escolas (Health in Schools)* programme.
CC   Ah, yes. We reintroduced a school nurse, and monthly check-ups for hearing, eyesight, teeth...
RP   We have provided a new methodology for teachers to deal with cognitive blockages, like psychological problems that derive from over-exposure to violence.
CC   If a programme is very expensive, too expensive to operate in all 1069 schools, we give it only to the Schools of Tomorrow. Some of these schools are CIEPs, and others are normal public schools. It's like an affirmative action scheme: we are very demanding with the kids, but we provide more help.

So are all the Schools of Tomorrow located in the most disadvantaged areas of Rio de Janeiro?

CC   Yes. The poorer and more violent areas. The Darcy Ribeiro Foundation are helping us with a programme for five very challenging schools—five CIEPs—in Maré, which is one of the most violent areas of the city. In some areas where violence is prevalent, the community still looks after the schools because their kids are studying there—even narcos have their kids. But in Maré, we still have problems with schools being invaded by outsiders at the weekends. The traffickers have a party every Saturday night where they sell drugs. But perhaps we can teach the community to better care for the CIEPs, as well as enhancing the teaching. It's about integrating the community; we want to recapture that original idea.

Last question: we learned recently that all CIEPs have been listed, meaning that the buildings are protected by law, they can't be modified. How do you think that might affect schools in the future?

CC   I have mixed feelings about that. It might freeze their evolution if we are not careful. On the other hand, the CIEPs are part of the state history. I don't know if we can freeze an idea forever, another group of people might rethink these ideas in the future. But then, I do like the idea of having the model frozen, do you know why? When I arrived here, the CIEPs were not fashionable, it was as if they had been a mistake. I don't believe they were a mistake. The ideas behind the CIEPs are very interesting. Darcy Ribeiro's idea, if I can sum it up in a few words, was that the elites provide their kids with going to movies, the theatre, travelling, they have doctors—and those kids that are in the CIEPs, they don't have access to anything of the kind. With the CIEPs, the idea was to bring a multi-sectoral approach to changing lives.
And this idea, it's magic. Even if in the beginning it was a little bit naïve, we have to recapture the good side of this naivety. The idea that it's possible to change the lives of these kids. If we don't believe in this, then why have public schools?

Detail from Aberrant Architecture's Animating Education installation, part of The British Pavillion at the Venice Biennale of Architecture in 2012

Can Good Architecture Be One-Size-Fits-All?
>Alastair Donald, David Chambers and Kevin Haley

What lessons can we learn from an unprecedented project in Brazil, which sought to standardise school architecture for Rio de Janeiro's quickly expanding education system? *Alastair Donald*, Architecture Program Manager at the British Council, and *David Chambers* and *Kevin Haley*, founding directors of *Aberrant Architecture*, debated the question in the wake of the Venice Architecture Biennale 2012.

The history of CIEPs and the lessons they hold for today were the focus for *'Lessons from Brazil: Is Standardised School Design Compatible with Architecture?'*, a panel discussion which took place at London's Royal Institute of British Architects (RIBA) headquarters, in conjunction with the exhibition Venice Takeaway: Ideas to Change British Architecture, commissioned for the Biennale by the British Council.

'It's a brave city that says, "Here is our standard school and we are building it everywhere."' Such was the response of *Mairi Johnson*, deputy design director of the Education Funding Agency, to the compelling story of the CIEPs (Integrated Centres of Public Education), an experimental educational project conceived in Rio de Janeiro, Brazil in 1982.

Pioneered by the then-State Governor Leonel Brizola along with his deputy, the intellectual Darcy Ribeiro, and designed by the world-renowned modernist architect Oscar Niemeyer, the CIEPs are a testament to ambition and forward thinking. They show the response of a city freeing itself from dictatorship while confronting the challenges of hyper-inflation, mass urban migration and a, previously unimaginable, full-time education programme for its citizens.

As part of their contribution to Venice Takeaway at the Biennale, *Aberrant Architecture* travelled to Brazil to investigate the CIEP school building programme, which remains relatively unknown outside of Brazil. Aberrant Architecture visited a number of schools that form part of the remarkable 508-strong network of CIEPs that cover the entire city and state of Rio de Janeiro, and which were built in just eight years.

In March 2013, a year on from that research trip, *Washington Fajardo*, president of the Rio World Heritage Institute—now leading a re-assessment of the CIEPs in anticipation of a new school construction programme in Rio—joined a panel of UK experts and a sold-out audience.

Standardisation in the UK: a Contentious Issue

With an urgent need to tackle the shortage of schools, in 2013 the UK was gearing up for a new school-building programme that embraced standardisation. However as noted by *Oliver Wainwright*, architecture critic for The Guardian, the very concept of standardisation has become contentious amongst some architects.

Janie Chesterton, education sector director at British architectural office Willmott Dixon, may have been right to point out that 'pre-design' is a more useful term than standardisation for efficient school design. Yet it remains inescapable that in the UK, at least, the very idea of 'standardised' building design for mass production widely connotes the image of cheap, poor quality, unambitious and uninspiring constructions, often critically referred to as 'Flat-Pack Schools', 'McSchools' or worse.

Beauty, Speed and Low Cost

Yet while standardisation may seem anti-design or even anti-architect, *Aberrant Architecture* argued that system building, properly developed with the involvement of architects, could provide avenues for school building that would combine scale and quality—as suggested by Fajardo's discussion of Rio's CIEPs. In a talk illustrated by Niemeyer's beautiful annotated sketches, Fajardo made it clear that a confident architect faces no contradiction between the needs of standardisation and the proposition of ambitious architecture.

Niemeyer clearly revelled in an architectural programme that reconciled beauty, speed of execution and low cost. Bold in appearance, unashamedly modernist in form and manufactured using factories capable of mass-producing up to sixty schools at a time, the CIEPs would appear an extremely brave approach from the perspective of today's risk-averse processes of public commissioning and procurement.

As *Sunand Prasad*, director of architectural practice Penoyre & Prasad remarked, it is a testimony that the CIEPs retain their emotional affect to this day: the symbolic products of an emerging democracy, from a state which was prepared to respond radically to its civic responsibility.

Customise and Multiply

In Brazil, this politically-charged outlook led to a school-building programme that pushed boundaries in every sense. According to Fajardo, confidence in the design, in the feasibility and in the social value of the overall project drove ambitious plans to both customise and multiply the schools.

Customisation ensured that the standard prefabricated system components could be fitted to various sites and cater to different school sizes. For example, smaller accessory buildings were added to larger school site in order to support the main school block, whereas smaller sites might see a clustering of functions.

Plans to multiply the programme across the state formed and reinforced a public infrastructural network, in which quality of environment and the ambition of the curriculum remained consistent in the CIEPs, whether in the wealthy south of metropolitan Rio de Janeiro, to the poorer western suburbs; or from way downtown to the North Zone favelas and more distant beach resorts. The standardised school—in Niemeyer's hands at least—brought design flair and a distinctive architectural identity to previously under-served locations, such that the design itself became a recognisable stamp, an ubiquitous symbol of high quality education.

As Fajardo outlined, not all aspects of the CIEPs programme worked perfectly, but many past design problems are informing the design of classrooms in new Brazilian programmes like the *Escolas do Amanhã* or Schools of Tomorrow. Today it seems clear, as it was to Niemeyer, that a modular system for educational buildings can readily accommodate well-designed interiors and exteriors, while maintaining a strong design character that engages with local contexts. 'Standardisation' is not the problem, but rather the fact that it could become a vehicle to deliver an ultimately modest, risk-averse and unambitious architecture.

What next for the UK?

In that sense, the question remained as to whether current plans for the UK employ too much standardisation—or perhaps, not enough? Undoubtedly, the chance to design several hundred primary schools would be a delicious challenge for Penoyre & Prasad— a practice which has distinguished itself in the design of hospitals, schools and other civic amenity buildings, and Willmott Dixon anticipated that construction of sixty schools at a time would certainly open up interesting possibilities for efficient procurement.

Can architects be confident that modular building at scale is compatible with high quality architecture? On this, the final word went to Sunand Prasad, who focussed on the loss of the 'architect as builder' and with this role, the loss of technical knowledge, which would allow the intelligent distillation of complex building programmes into a number of standardised components.

Architecture, he argued, has retreated, ceding the ground of technique, logistics and engineering to others. At a time when architecture is often reduced to box-ticking—not least within Britain's recent school building programmes—re-covering that lost ground could mark a useful way forward.

Alastair Donald is a Programme Manager for Architecture at the British Council, London. He joined the British Council as part of the curatorial team for the exhibition Venice Takeaway: Ideas to Change British Architecture, shown at the Venice Architecture Biennale in 2012 and in which Aberrant Architecture explored the CIEPs as part of their installation 'Animating Education'. Donald has advised on urban policy at the Office of the Deputy Prime Minister, and he is associate director of the Future Cities Project, which critically explores issues around the city and society.

Aberrant Architecture's Civic Stage in Swansea is influenced by the CIEPs, using strong form in conjunction with a loosely programmed civic space

Always More To Learn
                Aberrant Architecture

London, 2016

Dear Leonel, Oscar & Darcy,

We hope this greets you as friends from afar. For the past few years, we have been studying, visiting and speaking with many people who have contributed to the CIEPs schools. There are so many things we would like to ask you, but today we have tried to note the 'lessons' we have learned from your work.

    Like you, we hope to act as dreamers and designers of a better future. We work as architects, Oscar; our first encounter with the CIEPs project was visual, admiring the strong and distinctive buildings. Darcy, we also teach young people; when we first entered a CIEP school in Rio, it was wonderful to see children running around, empowered by their experience of education. And Leonel, we too have found education to be crucial in realising our successes; it means a lot to find such an ambitious project directed towards those who have less.

    Indeed, the most astonishing achievement was maintaining the ambition of such a socially generous project. We cannot imagine your optimism at the dawn of a new democratic era, or the challenges of choosing to serve these previously neglected masses at the risk of alienating traditional sources of power. With serious financial and temporal constraints, recognising the scale of the task and your socialist—even communist—tendencies, you must have known that you only had a short window in which to realise your goals.

Working Together

Perhaps it was thanks to these constraints, but we found it remarkable that the CIEPs engaged multiple team members, their various skills and contrasting ways of thinking. Darcy, were many of the spatial ideas actually yours? Oscar, did any pedagogical suggestions come from you? Did it really matter? Neither purely architectural, social or pedagogical, your collaborative mixing of traditional roles and hierarchies on this project seems more like a band making an album: not just 'Architect', 'Anthropologist', 'Engineer' or 'Client' but rather a group of variously talented musicians in the studio, jamming, swapping 'instruments' and enjoying the sounds that came out.

    Whether using storyboards like Oscar (indeed, as we do ourselves!) or through workshops and surveys, architects are often obliged to devise some kind of 'participation' involving clients or users—'stakeholders' as we say now—in the design process. It is incredible to think that you were already doing this, with teachers at the Mendes convention. More amazing is that these conversations did not stop with the completion of the buildings; the CIEPs became established as the heart of a lifelong learning programme, within the respective communities. Giving everyone—pupils, staff and local people—the opportunity to develop their skills collectively and participate in a wider conversation, still seems ahead of its time.

    This is something that we are trying to develop in our work today. You might be pleased to learn that we adopted a Mendes-like approach for our first school project. Of course it's on a much smaller scale, but we developed our brief for the redevelopment of *Rosemary Works Primary School* in London through a conversation with the entire school community: directors, teachers, administrative staff, children and parents, and we intend to keep working with them for several years.

Longevity and Value

In hindsight, you were right to spend money on a beautiful and strong infrastructure. If you want real change, it makes sense to build something truly permanent; while economy is important, it wouldn't make sense to use cheap materials for such a project. These days, young architects rarely get the chance to build much beyond the temporary: it's fun but you can't really make the same points about value and quality. The present teachers regret that the original CIEPs' curriculum did not run for long enough either, blaming political volatility.

Over time, an infrastructure like the CIEPs can support a variety of teaching methods, from those in vogue when the school was built to approaches that are yet to be imagined. Seen through the Structuralist lens of Herman Hertzberger, architecture can act like a permanent framework, in which changes to interior and exterior spaces occur in response to circumstance and requirements.

We wish you could witness how well your ideas and spaces have survived the test of time; with little maintenance, the robust concrete architecture easily allows for adaptation, like the spacious classrooms which can easily be carved up into smaller spaces. This in-built flexibility reaches another level in the outdoor areas, like the covered arcade and the multipurpose room. We watched the children play, exercising not only their bodies but also their creativity, reimagining concrete modules as worlds of their own. These really are our favourite spaces and the ones most valued by the community: it has been amazing to learn about all the uses and spatial qualities they offer—from dark to light, open to closed, public to private. The archival drawings suggest the use of the multipurpose room for community events—but did you ever imagine that anyone would choose to get married in a CIEP?

The Playground Piazza

You might not recognise the new way that children play—holding their phones, like the communicators on Star Trek, or sitting at personal computers—staring into screens and hardly running around at all. Our lives are increasingly 'virtual', which means that making the time and space for physical play has never been more important. The favelas of Rio can be cramped or otherwise constrained environments, especially for children. In the UK, commercial pressures combine with technological reliance and parental anxiety, to pose new kinds of threats towards the actual spaces of play.

At the CIEPs, the large playgrounds suggest that outside spaces are as important as the inside ones. But not only for the children: from a civic, social and urbanistic points of view, it was a collective masterstroke to design the CIEPs spaces to be used independently from the operation of the school itself. Spaces like the multipurpose court break the convention of a school as a shuttered fortress, acting like urban piazzas or town squares.

Perhaps playgrounds today can function as urban rooms, allowing the local community to appropriate spaces to meet, eat or simply pass time together. Indeed, in building our *Social Playground* installation in Liverpool, we found the act of play to be creatively fulfilling for adults too—allowing for new kinds of cooperation. Instead of the high street or the shopping centre, the school could position itself as a cultural centre for the local community. Reimagined in this way, the spaces of education can act as a mechanism of resistance, a counterpoint to the privatisation of the public realm.

Power To The Users

One important lesson to learn from the CIEPs includes the perils of politics—of realising a project under the flag of a particular party, and leaning towards popularity at the risk of divisiveness. The CIEP buildings and the ideals they tried to embody were neglected for years; the people who work there point to a particular political position, too far to the left to include the chorus that would be instrumental in sustaining the music that you began. From what we see in the present life of the CIEPs, the best way to ensure the longevity of your project is to give power and responsibility to its users and beneficiaries. One problem with relying on the state: you must rely on it to remain motivated in the same direction. But from what we saw, some CIEP communities feel themselves to be at least partly independent and indeed proud of managing their own affairs, within your monumental framework of concrete (and) ideals.

Setting New Standards

Learning from your trials, at *Rosemary Works Primary School* we designed a set of rules, rather than fixed solutions. Within these rules, the school and its users are empowered to make their own decisions, which they can agree on together. This follows your idea of flattening hierarchies, and allows the 'institution' to give way to the community. Within our design, we provided modular and adaptable components to animate the school's flexible hall space, borrowing from the success of the CIEPs' multipurpose room.

On an urban scale too, we take heart from the possibility of creating flexible, unprogrammed spaces; in fact we have tried to offer a new one to the city of Swansea, in Wales. The *Swansea Fitted Civic Stage* borrows the use of a graphically distinct form with a recognition of locally embedded histories, to provide a space where people might celebrate their expressions of urban collectivity.

The CIEPs project really revolutionised the way we think about standardisation. In the UK, prefabrication and modular systems have become synonymous with a lowly architecture of compromise. But the Brazilian context in which you worked showed us a new way of looking, at a scale that would be otherwise impossible, and a suggestion of equality across a radically divided society. Whilst no single school is the same, what is obvious is that fundamentally each one consists of the same elements, such as a classroom, staff room and a hall. In recent decades, we are sorry to say the world is only more divided; economic pressures increasingly dominate big decisions, but in your vision there are positive dimensions to standardised provision. Whilst the CIEPs used a kit of standardised parts as prefabricated design elements, some experts are now looking at standardising the connections rather than the components. Such an approach would allow for bespoke responses to any given site, with total freedom and flexibility in lengths, heights and angles of components; in the future, this modular way of thinking could be pushed even further. As Darcy said, there is always more to learn!

Well, we should probably end this letter here and keep learning through the inspiration of your work; through the limitations you tested and the successes of your collective ambition. It only remains to say thank you, for showing us how we might work together—architects, thinkers, politicians, children, humans—for a better future. Muito, muito obrigado.

Abraços,

David and Kevin

Beatrice Galilee is the Daniel Brodsky Associate Curator of Architecture and Design at the Metropolitan Museum of New York. As a curator, writer, consultant and lecturer she has worked prolifically and internationally, as chief curator of Close, Closer, the 2013 Lisbon Triennale of Architecture; co-curator of the 2011 Gwangju Design Biennale and the 2009 Shenzhen Hong Kong Bi-City Biennale of Architecture and Urbanism, and as curator of the experimental performance design projects Hacked (2012) and Afrofuture (2013) at Milan Design Week in Italy.

Postscript

Beatrice Galilee

While learning about the extraordinary achievements described in this book, under one of the most important architects of the 20th century, it is worth reflecting on the authors' position and the research strategies they have employed. It is no coincidence that much of this book, conceived and edited by *Aberrant Architecture*, takes the form of intimate conversations, with individuals whose voices and reflections are seldom heard.

Since its inception in 2010, *Aberrant* has been drawn to understanding the incidental relationships generated by design—or better still, understanding incidental design by examining the relationships it generates. During a residency at the Victoria and Albert Museum in London, David Chambers and Kevin Haley analysed the typology of the Victorian pub as a place of political, social and cultural exchange; this research was later used to design a playful, convivial pub table *(Devil Amongst the Tailors)*. After an investigation into 21st century working habits, *Aberrant* transformed an ailing restaurant into a successful co-working space, housing the *Gopher Hole*, an architecture gallery, underneath. Having since extended to schools, public art and performative projects, *Aberrant's* work is threaded through by an underlying concern, one which suggests that architectural practice should be simply rooted and clearly understood, as a manifestation of the myriad forces—problems or opportunities—that brought it to bear.

This thoughtful, timely book examines the luminous humanity of Oscar Niemeyer's lesser-known, standardised yet bespoke CIEP school buildings, allowing its readers to appreciate the roles played by Rio's politicians and anthropologists at the heart of a major educational experiment, and to understand this history through the voices of those who were there, who cared then, and who still care now. Essentially a prefabricated school system, the CIEPs' reach extended far beyond Niemeyer's concrete plasticity and flowed into public and pedagogical policy, family lives, and the broken communities of Rio's citizens. This book is an effort to explain and explore an holistic vision: a thorough, state-coordinated education for all, as a collaboration with the forces of power, and as lived through the experiences of those involved in this ambition.

As promised by the book's title, which credits politicians and intellectuals alongside the architect, the contemporary and historical conversations herein describe a complicated metaphorical and physical terrain, of the poverty and precarity experienced by communities living mostly in favelas. The constant presence of these iconic, intelligent and beautiful schools, some pock-marked by bullets, are a foil for the repeating narratives of frustrations echoed and counter-argued throughout. Clearly, there is a lack of nuance for the historic preservation of these 508 buildings, as well as lessons to be learned about the closeness of political ideology and symbolism, which ultimately lead to end of the CIEPs programme.

In 2016, the long-awaited Latin American Olympic Games finally arrived in Rio de Janeiro. But in what was supposed to be the city's golden year, international headlines were dominated by damning skepticism, either around the lack of a substantive social, environmental or urban legacy, or by the political crisis resulting in the impeachment of President Dilma Rousseff—not to mention the global panic around the Zika virus.

In its own small way, this publication offers a pivot back to Rio's radical and innovative history, and suggests what this complicated city has to offer not only to Brazil, but to any city hopeful to change its fortunes through listening and learning.

Acknowledgements

Aberrant Architecture is a multi-award winning collaborative studio of designers, makers and thinkers whose projects introduce new and unexpected ways of experiencing everyday life. Combining storytelling and research at the heart of their practice, Aberrant takes a playful approach to producing spatial experiences that are both meaningful and beautiful.

Aberrant's participatory form of practice places the needs of people at the centre of the problems they address and the opportunities they create. Aberrant design interactive architecture, interiors, public art, exhibitions & installations, building close relationships with the communities in which they operate.

Aberrant has exhibited work at international architecture exhibitions at the Venice Biennale of Architecture, Gwangju Design Biennale, Sao Paulo Biennial and the Hong Kong & Shenzhen Bi-City Biennale, and co-founded the Gopher Hole, an event space in London. Aberrant Architecture held the first architecture residency at the Victoria and Albert Museum (V&A); their work has been collected by the V&A and the Museum of Art in Rio de Janeiro.

Aberrant Architecture was founded by David Chambers and Kevin Haley in 2010.

Acknowledgements
Aberrant Architecture

First of all, we would like to thank the Graham Foundation for Advanced Studies in the Fine Arts for kindly supporting this publication and the British Council for supporting our research. We are grateful to Paulo Herkenhoff and Vicky Richardson for their generous comments, which persuaded the Foundation to back this project.

We are particularly indebted to Fernanda Balata for her boundless interest and excitement for the project, carrying out so many of the interviews and research as well as acting as both trip coordinator, translator, transcriber, photographer, general sounding board and all-round enthusiast from the very beginning.

We must also thank Christina Becker, James Chambers, Alastair Donald, Washington Fajardo, Vanessa Norwood, Pedro Rivera, all our interviewees and all of the CIEPs' students, staff, friends and colleagues who kindly gave their time and thoughts towards this book.

We would also thank our contributors Beatrice Galilee, Ligia Nobre, Shumi Bose and Vicky Richardson, as well as our team of translators and transcribers, Fernanda De Almeida Castelo Branco, Paula Lobato and Manuela Leal.

Thanks goes to graphic designer Tom Lobo Brennan; to Hara Anastasiou for her beautiful illustrations; the Fundação Darcy Ribeiro and the Fundação Oscar Niemeyer for letting us have access to such amazing archival drawings and images, and to Simon Kennedy for his stunning photography.

Finally, there are those who were just instrumental in making things happen in Rio. There are so many to mention but we are much obliged to Tathiana Balata and Bruno Maciel for driving us to so many different CIEPs, and to Marta and Fernando Balata for hosting us and keeping us fuelled with delicious food. This book simply could not have happened without all of your help; like the CIEPs themselves, it is a project of many hands.

Thank you all,

David and Kevin
Aberrant Architecture, 2016

Concept
David Chambers & Kevin Haley
(Aberrant Architecture)

Editing
David Chambers, Kevin Haley,
Fernanda Balata

Graphic Design
Tom Lobo Brennan

Translation & Editorial Assistance
Fernanda Balata, Fernanda De Almeida
Castelo Branco, Paula Lobato,
Manuela Leal

Illustrations
Aberrant Architecture
with Hara Anastasiou

Lithography, Printing, and Binding
DZA Druckerei zu Altenburg GmbH,
Altenburg

© 2016 David Chambers, Kevin Haley
and Park Books AG, Zurich
© for the texts: the authors
© for the images: see image credits

Despite best efforts, we have not been able to identify the holders of copyright and printing rights for all the illustrations. Copyright holders not mentioned in the credits are asked to substantiate their claims, and recompense will be made according to standard practice.

Park Books AG
Niederdorfstrasse 54
8001 Zurich
Switzerland

www.park-books.com
All rights reserved; no part of this work may be reproduced or edited using electronic systems, copied, or distributed in any form whatsoever without previous written consent from the publisher.

ISBN 978-3-03860-026-8

Image Credits
pp. 01, 22, 112, 114, 116, 120: illustration © Aberrant Architecture with Hara Anastasiou
pp. Cover (front & back), 02, 24, 36, 49 (top), 90, 94, 108, 188 (bottom): image © Fundação Darcy Ribeiro. Published under authorisation.
pp. 6, 8, 12, 18, 42, 47, 49 (bottom), 58, 64, 67, 76, 79, 80, 83, 86, 98, 104, 106, 122, 124, 126, 134, 136, 141, 142, 145, 147, 153, 154, 156, 158, 162, 168, 170, 173, 174, 176, 178: image © Aberrant Architecture.
pp. 11, 184: image © Cristiano Corte
pp. 28, 188 (top): image © Simon Kennedy
p. 40: image © Ana Nascimento/ABr - Agência Brasil
pp. 60, 68. 70, 72, 96, 100: © Fundação Oscar Niemeyer. Published under authorisation.
p. 62: image © Zoran Milich/Alamy

Printed on Munken Lynx Rough (FSC/PEFC Certified)

The typeface used within this book is called Souvenir and Neue Haas Unica. Souvenir was the typeface that was used in 'O Livro Dos Cieps', (Bloch Editores S.A, 1986), a book intended to act as a manual for the CIEPs initiative.

This publication was made possible with the generous support of:

Graham Foundation